Laughter At The Wicket

Harry East

Echoes from the Golden Age of
Yorkshire Cricket

The Whitethorn Press Limited

Dedicated...

to my wife, bless her, who, I calculate, has spent her last 1,028 summer Saturday afternoons bored to distraction in village cricket fields, waiting anxiously for the refreshment tent shutter to be raised so that she could dash off for a cup of tea and a gossip.

Litho Preparation by Lapex Printing Ltd.
Heswall, Wirral.
Printed by Gibbons Barford, Wolverhampton
for the publishers, The Whitethorn Press Ltd.,
Thomson House, Withy Grove, Manchester M60 4BL

© Harry East 1980

ISBN 0 9506055 7 3

Contents

Prologue 7
The Star of the North 9
The Auctioneer from Thirsk 13
The Handloom Weyvers 16
The Father of the Flock 19
Test Hero Who Never Played 23
O my Jackson and my Leyland 26
The Comic from Halifax 29
The Chapel-goer 32
Super Boss 35
The Perfect Bowler 41
The Greatest County Cricketer of All Time 45
Hero of Mafeking 48
The Governor of Bengal 51
The off-comed Chucker 55
O my Emmett and my Wainwright 58
Neglected Hero 61
Mastermind 63
The Likely Lad from Lawkholme 67
Immaculate Bulwark 71
The 'Cross Bat Village Greener' 75
Epilogue 77

Acknowledgements

My sincere thanks are due to Mrs. B. G. Howard for allowing me to use photographs of her father, H. J. Knutton; to the late Arnie Mosley, of East Bierley Cricket Club, and Edwin Wright, of Buttershaw Congs. Cricket Club, captains of my youth, who taught me that cricket was fun; to the hundreds of old Yorkshiremen with whom, during the last fifty years, I have sat under drystone walls listening enthralled to their cricket wisdom; to the editors of *Yorkshire Life, The Yorkshire Observer* and the *Yorkshire Ridings Magazine* for permission to use material already published; and lastly, and most importantly, to Maurice Colbeck, without whose interest, advice and generous help, this book would never have been written.

HARRY EAST

In addition to those named above, the publishers wish to thank the following for permission to reproduce photographs, etc.: BBC Hulton Picture Library (Tom Emmett, p. 59; Schofield Haigh, cover and p. 60): Central Press and Telegraph and Argus (Emmott Robinson p. 68; Maurice Leyland p. 74); Mr. Norman Hazell (Wilfred Rhodes, Herbert Sutcliffe and Lord Hawke, cover, pp. 26 and 64): MCC (Haigh, Hirst and Rhodes, p. 8; Fuller Pilch, p. 11; Schofield Haigh, p. 27; Tom Emmett, p. 28; Ted Peate, p. 40); Telegraph and Argus (Maurice Leyland p. 27); Yorkshire Post (W.G. Grace, p. 58; Herbert Sutcliffe, p. 72).

In a few cases sources of quotations have been difficult to trace. We apologise for any unintentional infringement and will be glad to make due acknowledgement in future editions.

Pencil drawings by Edward Bates
Cartoons by Ernest Andrew

PROLOGUE

I'm told they play cricket in other places besides Yorkshire. On reflection, I realize that they must, otherwise we should have nobody to beat. But these others are a weak, insipid, puerile lot – at least in our eyes.

There are few foreigners whom we respect: W. G. Grace, naturally, for he had more monkey tricks up his sleeve than all the Yorkshire cricketers who ever played, all put together; Don Bradman, who twice came to Leeds and scored over 300 in a Test match; Sydney Barnes, who in almost a decade of league cricket took about a hundred wickets a year at an average of around four runs each, when his opponents included Jack Hobbs, Frank Woolley and George Gunn. But most of all we revere dear old Tom Hunt, for Tom came from Chesterfield to Yorkshire and saw that it was good, and settled amongst us and took up our native game. And so expert did he become at single wicket cricket that in 1845, alone, he played Eleven of Knaresborough, and beat them, scoring 23 and 10 in his two innings and bowling Knaresborough out for 16 and nine. And of Knaresborough's 25 runs 14 were wides, so that 22 batsmen made only 11 runs between them.

The game was scheduled for the 6th, 10th and 14th of August, but, sadly, says a report, 'There was no play on the 10th, although all the players were present. The Knaresborough umpire was intoxicated and there was nobody else available'.

Alas, poor Tom! He learnt more from the old Yorkshire stalwarts than how to play cricket. After a convivial evening with his cricketing cronies it was his practice, in spite of dire warnings to walk home along the railway track. One night, either he was early or the train was late. And that was the end of him.

So let us now praise famous men, but for a moment, before we start, pay tribute to those whom fame spurned, whose talents were prodigious, but to whom opportunity was forbidden.

Let us think of Irvine Greenwood, who, if he could have bent in the field, might have nipped Maurice Leyland's career in the bud; of Cecil Tyson whose scores in his first match for Yorkshire were 100 not out and 80 not out, but who could not get his release from a Saturday afternoon professional engagement; of Arthur Booth, who, in his only full season for Yorkshire, when well over 40 years of age, topped the All England bowling averages; of Joseph Preston, who first played for Yorkshire in 1883 at the age of 19 and who, 'had he possessed the least self restraint might have become one of the finest cricketers Yorkshire ever produced'; of Major Booth and Alonzo Drake, whom war and illness cut down in their prime when they had given evidence, in 1913 and 1914, of becoming the greatest pair of opening bowlers in the world; of Horace Fisher, doyen of Yorkshiremen playing as a Saturday afternoon professional in the Lancashire Leagues.

Bowling at Lord's against Middlesex, Horace hit Patsy Hendren on the pads, but his loud appeal for leg before wicket was turned down. 'Nay', said Horace to the umpire in disgust, 'yong theer 'Endren were fair anent.' There was neither response nor castigation. The umpire didn't speak foreign languages.

And, finally, poor Albert Cordingley. In 1897 Bobby Peel had been dismissed from the Yorkshire team. At the start of the 1898 season Albert had been pencilled in to replace Bobby as Yorkshire's slow left arm bowler. Before the first match in 1898 Cordingley and another colt, who was already in contact with Warwickshire, were given a net. But Albert didn't bowl straight and the other colt, the second string, was given a run in the match against Marylebone Cricket Club. Poor Albert. The stand-by was Wilfred Rhodes. If only Albert had bowled straight! So although my title is 'Laughter at the Wicket' the laughter is often close to tears.

But enough of tragedy . . . Let us now turn to those whom Fortune blessed with her skill, as did Nature with her greatest birthright, that of being born Yorkshiremen.

Three of those 'whom Fortune blessed with her skill, as Nature bestowed her greatest birthright, that of being Yorkshiremen' – Schofield Haigh, George Hirst and Wilfred Rhodes – 'taken at Blake Lee, Marsden, October 21, 1905'.

STAR OF THE NORTH

There is a story that as the future Lord Montgomery was being driven to the aerodrome to fly out and take command of the Eighth Army, he mused to himself as follows . . . 'It seems a great shame. A man dreams from childhood of a military career. He passes, with honour, through Staff College. By energy, determination and industry he attains high rank, and then, all his service and years of dedication are snuffed out and reduced to nought because he comes up against one of the greatest military geniuses the world has ever known.'

'Oh, come', said the officer who was driving, 'you might not find it as bad as all that.'

'I wasn't thinking about myself', answered Monty in some surprise. 'I was feeling sorry for Rommel.'

Of such a breed was Tom Marsden, the Sheffield cricketer. A famous left-hand batsman and dual purpose bowler (very fast underhand or medium round-arm) he challenged the world. He was landlord of the 'Cricketers' at Darnall and offered to pull down the sign of his inn if anyone could beat him at single wicket cricket.

In 1828 he had sent the following letter to the *Sheffield Independent*, 'Sir, You will please to state in your next paper that my friends are ready to back me to play any man in England a match at single wicket for the sum of £50. The game to be played on the New Ground at Darnall on Monday, the 13th or Monday, the 20th of October; and the person accepting the challenge to receive £10 for his travelling expenses. Upon receiving an answer to this challenge, the stakes will be immediately sent to your office.' But nobody accepted his challenge, and later, in *Bell's Life*, he caused to be published,

'Knurr and Spell.

'Tom Marsden, of Sheffield, will play any man at this game at the close of the cricketing season for £50 or £100. Each man to choose his own knurrs.'

It was not surprising that his cricket challenge was unaccepted. In 1826, when Sheffield played Nottinghamshire and the visitors scored 101 in their first innings and 75 in their second, Sheffield replied with 379 and of these, Marsden, batting for eight hours, scored 227. In those days of bumpy pitches and rough, unmown outfields, even 50 was regarded as a prodigious individual score.

Only 21 years old at the time, Marsden was hero-worshipped in South Yorkshire. A poet commemorated his innings in a rhyme of 13 stanzas, the chorus, 'Hey, Derry, Derry', being sung whenever the bibulous choristers in the local pubs wished to show their enthusiasm and appreciation . . .

Then Marsden went in, in his glory and pride,
  And the arts of the Nottingham players defied.
Oh! Marsden at cricket is Nature's perfection
  For hitting the ball in any direction.
He ne'er fears his wicket, so safely he strikes,
  And he does with the bat and the ball as he likes.

The poem ended . . .
> So for Kettleband quickly we made a good shout
>   But Tom, turning round, said let him look out;
> Then he drove the ball right over the people,
>   Some thought it were going over Handsworth church steeple.
> Then homeward I trudged to our county folks
>   To tell 'em a few of our cricketers' jokes.
> But that joke of Tom Marsden's will ne'er be forgot,
>   When two hundred and twenty-seven notches he got.
> For Marsden and Gamble we filled up our glasses
>   As brimful as when we toast favourite lasses;
> And then drank success to all cricketers true
>   Who with honour this noble diversion pursue.

Kettleband, who is mentioned, was the unfortunate Nottingham boundary fielder and Gamble a Sheffielder who took part with Marsden in a long stand.

A public subscription after the match raised £50 and provided Marsden with a silver cup to commemorate his score.

His challenge in the *Sheffield Independent* was at last accepted in 1830 by G. Jarvis, but Marsden won, and later, to show his skill and impartiality, he won a game in which 'bowling, throwing and jerking were allowed to be fair.'

It was strange that while Marsden, in Sheffield, was the greatest cricketer in the world, as soon as he left his native city he was as ineffectual as Samson shorn of his locks. Whenever he played in the South of England, he was invariably a failure, and in 1832, Pierce Egan's *Book of Sports* sarcastically said,
> Next Marsden may come, tho' it here must be stated,
>   That his skill down at Sheffield is oft over-rated.

His career was to end in ignominy. A rollicking fellow, he was burned out by the time he was twenty-five. And then, from the shadows where he had been lurking, his nemesis appeared.

Fuller Pilch, of Norwich, was a mighty cricketer (he will go down in history for, among other feats, having carried a scythe around with his cricket gear to mow the outfield before the match began). In 1828 Pilch had seen fit to ignore the gauntlet thrown down in the *Sheffield Independent*. Then, in 1833, Pilch challenged Marsden for the championship of England and £100 a side. Now, though Marsden was only a shadow of his former self, two matches were arranged, one at Norwich, the other at Sheffield. For Yorkshiremen they make sorry reading.

AT NORWICH
Marsden (first innings) 41 balls, 33 hits. 7 runs. Extras 0. Total 7
Marsden (second innings) 7 balls, 5 hits. 0 runs. Extras 0. Total 0
Pilch (first innings) 131 balls, 113 hits. 73 runs. Extras 4. Total 77 runs.
Pilch won by an innings and 70 runs.

AT SHEFFIELD
Pilch (first innings) 198 balls. 152 hits. 78 runs. 4 wides. Total 82 runs.
Pilch (second innings) 202 balls. 148 hits. 100 runs. 6 wides. Total 106 runs.
Marsden (first innings) 73 balls. 60 hits. 25 runs. 1 wide. Total 26 runs.

Marsden (second innings) 184 balls. 122 hits. 31 runs. 4 wides. Total 35 runs.
Pilch won by 127 runs.

In 1843, when he was only 38, Tom died. He was the last of Yorkshire's great single wicket champions. So great was his local fame and so revered his memory that two years after his death Mr. Clarke of the Leeds Cricket Club was presented with 'an elegant gold breast pin in token of respect for his services as treasurer'. The pin represented a bat, stumps and ball, but gruesome as it may seem in retrospect, instead of a gold or silver fastener, the chain was 'two links of the late Tom Marsden's hair'.

Fuller Pilch, who carried a scythe to mow the outfield before the match began.

George Freeman 'The terror of Lancashire . . .'

THE AUCTIONEER FROM THIRSK

On the first morning of the match at Sheffield Park in 1896, Ernie Jones, the Australian chucker, slung the ball full toss through Dr. W. G. Grace's beard.

Now this may not be as remarkable a feat as, at first sight, it seems, for the Doctor's beard, like that of Moses, was long and full and descended almost to his navel. In fact, it was reported at the time by malicious tongues, that a claim for leg before wicket might have been upheld if the Australians had been bold enough, in spite of the Doctor's fulminating complaints and strictures, to appeal.

Grace, although a Bristolian, was until recently, 90 years after his heyday, greatly admired by Yorkshiremen. (He was also greatly admired by Yorkshire ladies, for he was a famous waltzer, but we shall not press that angle of his accomplishments here.) I knew an old man at Savile Town, Dewsbury, whose greatest claim to fame, in his own opinion, was that, in 1910, he bowled out Charlie Chaplin for a duck, and spent the next fifty years in bewilderment wondering how anyone could flick a cane with such élan yet fail to hold a bat straight. This same veteran would lead you surreptitiously to a distant iron fence and point proudly to a railing. 'That', he would say, 'were bent back like that when one of Grace's sixes landed fair on it in . . .' And he would mention a date long before Queen Victoria's Jubilee had been anticipated. Being a Yorkshireman, he would conclude his tale by adding, 'But that six lost Gloucestershire t'match. They put Saul Wade on for t'next over and he bowled Grace first ball'.

And in a churchyard in Halifax is a headstone to the memory of William Gilbert Gill, who 'died on November 1st, 1975, aged 82 years'. He was a cattle dealer, travelling by van to all the marts of Yorkshire. 'Hev yo' a minute, Gilbert?' I importuned him one day when he was old and frail. And when he stopped, I continued, 'Was thy father a cricketer?' 'Aye', he said, 'he laiked in t'Airedale and Wharfedale League.' 'And who did he christen thee after?' He smiled, half proudly, half timidly, 'W. G. Grace', he said.

The Yorkshire admiration for Grace stemmed from his fearlessness. On all the treacherous, bumpy, bouncing pitches of the 19th century, when Kortright, Knox, Richardson, Mold, Sammy Woods and Demon Spofforth slung their thunderbolts at flinching batsmen, the Doctor stood four-square, hammering their cricket hearts to destruction. In one afternoon at Lord's in 1883 he killed the cricket career of 'Shoey' Harrison from Bowling Old Lane. Harrison had made a meteoric rise as a fast bowler and, in May, was chosen for the North versus the South Colts at Lord's. In a letter Harrison recalls the match: 'Our secretary asked me if I'd ever been to London before and when I told him Nay he replied, "Then thou'll hev to be very careful, cos there's a lot o' funny chaps knocks about Seven Dials and Petticoat Lane and if they get hold o' thee they'll tak' all thou has".'

However, apparently unmolested by the spivs of the day, he arrived at Lord's, but, such was the lack of communication in those days, nobody knew what he had come for. When it came to the second innings of the Southern Colts the Northern captain said to Harrison, 'What are you here for young man?' 'I'm here to bowl', said Shoey, 'and I'll bowl if thou'll put me on.'

Harrison's letter goes on, 'So he did and I got nine wickets for fourteen runs, hitting the stumps every time, taking four in successive balls, then a ball, then two other wickets in successive balls, making six wickets in seven balls'.

But his nemesis was to come later. In the Gentlemen versus Players match, Grace said to his opening partner, 'I've not seen this colt. Let me take the first over against him'. And in one afternoon Grace literally killed Shoey's cricket career, thrashing him mercilessly. Immediately play ended Harrison went straight to bed and never again was he of much use to the Yorkshire side.

But for one fast bowler, if he did not fear him, Grace had an awed respect, the Yorkshireman, George Freeman, and the other Yorkshire players knew it. Once, after Grace had scored over 300 against Twenty-two of Grimsby, when all his opponents had fielded, Grace came to play against Yorkshire. Up to him sidled Tom Emmett. 'Ee, Doctor', he chortled, 'thou'rt nooan laiking ageean cockle hawkers today. George'll show thee.'

Between George and the Doctor there had been a great match at Lord's in 1870. C. E. Green, a well known M.C.C. cricketer, showed Lord Hawke, in 1917, the mark of a blow where George had hit him that day long ago. Of the match in 1870, Grace said it was one of the roughest and bumpiest pitches he had ever known. And Tom Emmett doubted, after the match, if W. G. had a square inch of sound flesh on his body. George Freeman himself admitted that it was a marvel the Doctor was neither maimed nor unnerved for the rest of his days, or even killed outright . . . But, such was the antagonism between the two, not an inch did Grace retreat, nor did Freeman abate one iota his fearful pace or menacing bounce.

Neither in height nor physique was George outstanding, and, in his private life at Thirsk, he was a kind and gentle man. He had long, wavy black hair, sideburns and a shapely, curly moustache, making him look much like the straight man in a concert party. But in public life he was a mighty demolisher. By profession he was an auctioneer. At the West Riding cattle markets he knocked down the Shorthorn heifers and Herdwick and Swaledale sheep that the farmers brought to his hammer. And for fun in his spare time, garbed in a flamboyant striped shirt, he flattened with glorious fury and abandon the wickets of all who dared to hold their bats before him.

He first entered the Yorkshire team because of a strike. In 1866 Yorkshire's star players, Anderson, Atkinson, Iddison, Rowbotham and Stephenson, had refused to play against Surrey because they suspected that Surrey had instructed their umpire to no-ball them and George Anderson had refused to accept the captaincy of Yorkshire, declaring that he would not play 'against those who would have combined to sweep us from the cricket field altogether if they could'.

Refusing to give way to malcontents, the county committee decided to 'play the match with such talent as they could bring together at the risk of almost certain failure and pecuniary loss'. The feud lasted about 18 months. Among those drafted into the team as makeshifts during that period was Freeman, and he began by taking four wickets for 29 runs against Cambridgeshire at Bradford.

In the following year, 1867, he leapt to the forefront of England's bowlers, taking 51 wickets at 7.4 runs for the county. Three times Lancashire were defeated; by an innings and 56 runs, by 165 runs, and by an innings and 40 runs.

Freeman was the terror of Lancashire. At Whalley in 1867 he took seven wickets for 10 runs against them, and in 1868 at Holbeck eight wickets for 11 runs in the first innings and four wickets for 12 runs in the second.

In the All England bowling averages he was third in 1867, fifth in 1868, fifth in 1869 second in 1870 and top in 1871.

In 1872, when he was only 27, he retired. Business had lured the 'Prince of Bowlers' from the cricket fields of England. Like a comet he had made his sudden and vivid appearance and then disappeared. Vanished? Well, almost. Occasionally he was lured back, but the verve and excitement had gone. He seemed disenchanted with his former glory, remembered, perhaps, only by W. G. Grace from his youth. At the end of a career spanning 50 years W. G. admitted that George was the fastest of the lot.

In England both he and his feats have been forgotten. One hundred years is a long time. His memory and his bowling have faded, but in Canada his reputation will live for ever.

In 1868 he toured the dominion, played in six matches, all against odds, and took 126 wickets at the incredible average of 1.75 runs per wicket. His bowling and that of Arthur Appleby resulted a year or two later in a musical composition, *The Song of the Fast Bowler,* to be sung to the tune of the Canadian Boat Song, *Row, brothers, row.*

It runs to six stanzas, three of which read:
Stand to your stumps, the toss is won;
   I shall bowl you all out 'ere the day is done;
Breathes the Kanuk who can withstand
   The ball as it leaves my big left hand?
Field, brothers, field, my rapids are near
   To the sticks, and the shooters a way will clear.

Rose may bowl at the other end;
   May the breeze I spurn his slows befriend.
No matter to me, if against the hill,
   I am told to bowl, why, bowl I will!
Field, brothers, field, my rapids are near
   To the sticks, and the shooters a way will clear.

One on the knuckles! The wicket's rough,
   Another on the shins; they cry enough!
Middle stump, off stump, into mid-air,
   I can drop her short if to swipe they dare.
Field, brothers, field, my rapids are near
   To the sticks, and the shooters a way will clear.

THE HANDLOOM WEYVERS

It has become a fancy in travel and topographical books on the North of England to include an evening photograph of the textile mills at Milnsbridge, near Huddersfield, windows agleam, working shifts.

Whether the photograph is meant to impress the stranger with the mightiness of the textile trade or to demonstrate the stratagems to which we've been reduced in producing the necessities of export and, therefore, of existence, is never stated. However, any impression that may be created that night working is an unpleasant novelty of modern life is, of course, completely false. But the lights have increased in number, have stopped flickering as once they did, and have descended from the hill villages to the valleys.

It was the blustering rainy climate, the barren, shallow soil, the moors and waste land that caused the folk of the Pennine hills, to seek a living from sheep rearing and weaving home-grown wool. Although power looms became common in the nineteenth century, handloom weaving of fancy waistcoating and other intricate fabrics, continued as a male occupation, and not as a fanciful art, right to the turn of the century.

The tediousness and sedentary nature of the job were irksome to high spirits, and as each man was his own master, the tempting summer view of rolling hills and sun-kissed meadows from the long window of the upper chamber where he was struggling with some intricate pattern was often too strong. He would throw his shuttle aside and dash off to the moors, the cricket field or the knurr and spell course.

At night the uncompleted warp and the emptiness of his pocket would torment him back to work. With a guttering candle stuck at each end of his loom he would struggle in the gloomy light, confusing the colourings of his weft in the dimness and the dancing shadows, and berating himself a score of times for his frailty in the forenoon.

And the flickering lights in the garret windows would twinkle in the valleys, and the millhands of the power looms would smile as each man's dereliction of duty was illuminated for all the town to see.

It was the introduction of railway travel, the love of gambling endemic in these hill people, and the northward spread of cricket that showed them a more congenial way of making money than the interminable weaving.

Cricket matches for heavy sidestakes were arranged. Afternoons were given up to practice and playing. The people of the valley had no need to inquire who had won. Shouts of revelry and triumph from one village, twinkling garret lights from another, where the losers were trying feverishly to recoup the side stake, showed how the match had gone.

By the 1870s the hamlet of Lascelles Hall, perched on a hillside just outside Huddersfield, within sight of the fortress from which the Brigantes had hurled back the Roman invaders, emerged undisputed champions, and, for a decade, was to be the most incredible breeding ground of cricket champions the world had ever known.

Half the male population were professional cricketers. In 1877 Lascelles Hall provided the following professionals for the clubs mentioned: J. Ambler, Dalton; J. Castle, Haslingden; A. Eastwood, Redcar; L. Greenwood, Wakefield; W. Hardy, Kelso; H. Kaye, Saddleworth; J. Lockwood, Bolham; D. Pollard, Winchester and Harrow; T. Redfearn, Doncaster; John Thewlis, Birstall; Joseph Thewlis, Wakefield; T. Thewlis, Kendal; S. Wilson, Huddersfield, and, strangest of all, H. Lockwood, Casey's Clowns (whoever they might have been). And, in the same year, seven natives of the village played in the Yorkshire county team.

Though not dressed in the nankeen knee breeches and silk stockings which were considered the correct attire at Lord's and the universities, they became the terrors of the North of England.

Townships and cities fell before the prowess of this small hamlet. In one year four natives of the village played together in the prestigious Gentlemen versus Players match. Money challenges were flung far and wide. This segregated little community, which rarely left the precincts of its village except to play cricket, scourged the rest of Yorkshire.

Dalton cricketers, 1833 to 1903.

Victories would be celebrated with orgies of feasting and impromptu song.
Oh, the Sheffielders, they were the chaps to play at bat and ball,
But they could not beat the eleven lads that came from Lascelles Hall thundered the chorus to every stanza of the song commemorating a mighty victory for a huge side-stake. It is not by mere chance that Huddersfield has such a fine Choral Society, that the Mrs. Sunderland Music Festival has earned such renown, or that disgruntled supporters, even today, one hundred years after, still say of an unsuccessful professional from Huddersfield, 'They must hav signed 'im 'cos 'e can sing t'Holmfirth Anthem'.

In the seventies Lascelles Hall reached its zenith. They beat the Rest of Yorkshire, they beat Surrey, they played honourable draws with the North of England and with Parr's All England Eleven.

County cricket was becoming rationalised, side-stake matches fell into disrepute and, in 1877, more than half the Yorkshire team was Lascelles Hall men.

Even this, according to rumour, did not include the best cricketer the village ever produced. Years later, when Yorkshire were doing badly, failing to score runs, Lord Hawke approached George Hirst for advice. 'T'best batter in t'world laikes for Lascelles Hall', said George, 'but I'm flaid he likes his ale too mich to suit Your Lordship.'

Thus, it appeared, all Yorkshire revered Lascelles Hall, but this eulogizing was not echoed by its neighbouring hilltop village of Dalton. Here they will sniff at the mention of its fame. 'It were a pack of Dalton chaps who went to play there because they couldn't get into t'first team here', they will aver. They will point to their own formation in 1831, twenty-five years before Lascelles Hall, and will talk with pride of the Crossland brothers: 'They nivver hed nowt like t'Crosslands at Lascelles Hall.'

In 1852, Bendigo, the boxing champion of England, who was making a new name for himself at single wicket cricket, threw down the gauntlet against any man in the country. Andrew Crossland was in no hurry to accept. He waited till the side stakes had been increased to a substantial sum, then took up the challenge. Crossland batted first and was making a huge score when a dog seized one of his hits and ran away with the ball. Bendigo, seeing an opportunity of saving his money, became indignant, saying he had contracted to play against men, not dogs. He refused to continue and the match had to be abandoned. And, since Bendigo was the bare knuckle champion of England, perhaps even such a mighty warrior as Andrew Crossland was wise not to offer to 'feyt him for it'.

These Crossland brothers had supreme confidence in their own skill. In 1850 Dalton played an All England Eleven and, at the end of the first day, famous old George Parr was 99 not out. Long odds were laid in the ale houses that night on George getting his hundred, and the Crosslands were happy to accept. The following morning Johnny Crossland had him caught in the first over without scoring, and he and Andrew proceeded to collect from side bets more than their handlooms would have earned them in the whole of the season.

They have little esteem for Lascelles Hall at Dalton till you couple the two villages. Then they will smile proudly. 'Ee, lad', they will say, 'if Lascelles Hall and Dalton had nobbut joined together, nivver mind abaht t'Rest of England, they'd hev beaten t'Rest of t'World.'

FATHER OF THE FLOCK

Probably, and no doubt he would have been vastly disgruntled if any other claimant to the honour had usurped him, Ikey Hodgson was the worst batsman and most slovenly fielder who ever lived.

But nobbut just. His bosom pal, Billy Slinn, ran him a close second. Once, unfortunately, early in his career, when he was raw and unsophisticated, Billy had twice scored double figures in the same match. In the total there would be snicks through the slips which butter-fingered fieldsmen had failed to accept; there would be shots that had bounced in eccentric, non-geometric orbits from a wavering, horizontal bat to points unknown in the glossary of fieldsmanship. Nevertheless, whether through accident or design, and all available evidence points to the former, Billy had suffered the indignity of being unable to prevent the ball and his bat coming into contact often enough, so that ten had twice been registered against his name.

No such misdemeanour ever sullied Ikey's escutcheon. He was not a cricketer. To him, batting and fielding were, as far as personal participation was concerned, distasteful chores to be avoided or, at worst, evil necessities that the idiosyncracies of the game demanded, and were to be undertaken with the minimum of interest and effort. Had that multitude of iniquitous forms that sift into our private lives been in existence 150 years ago, he would have entered, 'Isaac Hodgson; born November 15th, 1828, in the township of Bradford; occupation, professional bowler'.

Or more likely he would have ignored it and been sought by tipstaff and bailiff. They would not have found him, for Ikey was the peripatetic opponent, the shadow of William Clarke's All England XI, the haunter and nightmare of his batsmen.

'The best man for a XXII now living', a critic pronounced him when he was sweeping, like the sword of Gideon, through the ranks of the tourists' champions. Not, mark you, for an eleven. No team of any standing could afford to include Ikey and Billy, to see their last wicket fall at number eight and to field nine players. Once, in a moment of desperation, the United All England XI had invited their co-operation, but in six innings they made a grand total of one run. There is no record extant of the number of catches they dropped or gently bouncing balls they failed to gather, but, it seems, the sad conclusion was reached that their talents were outweighed by their imperfections and the invitations ceased.

But, for a XXII, their very failings were their virtues. With 22 fieldsmen to disseminate, the ground was reminiscent of Piccadilly Circus on Mafeking night, and sixth or seventh longstop were acceptable posts to Ikey and Billy.

A village captain, faced with the unenviable necessity of making out his batting order, risked a vendetta of Corsican bitterness by being compelled to insult one of the rustics by requesting, 'Wilt thou go in at t'fall of twentieth wicket, Isaiah?'

Ikey and Billy lifted that burden from his shoulders. There was no need to tell them. They never looked at the score book or the list of names pinned behind the dressing tent door. Twenty-first and twenty-second were their positions by right, by usage, by custom, and whether precedence was decided by rote, by tossing a coin, by alphabetical order or by seniority was a matter of indifference. In the polite language of the time they rarely 'troubled the scorers' and would probably have lost their way if they had been compelled to cross the wicket.

William Clarke (known as Old Clarke) was a famous cricketer, a native of Nottingham. He once invited the Sheffield Cricket Club to meet Nottingham for £500, with the suggestion that the stumps should be pitched 'half way between Sheffield and Nottingham, each party bearing its own expenses'; for besides being a man of mighty deeds Old Clarke was a great lover of money.

So he assembled his All England XI playing anywhere, town or village, where he could be guaranteed a 'gate', often taking on 18 or 22 opponents and the two 'home' umpires as well. And, being a man of great cunning, he laid as many side bets as possible with the village yokels, who, when their bellies were full of ale, were apt to think that the sun shone out of their village heroes.

After the match, his top hat brimming with golden sovereigns, Old Clarke assembled his men in the local pub, rewarded them scantily from his fortune, and, if they murmured in dissatisfaction at their miserly stipend, advised them to 'take their hooks back home'. There were plenty more in the South and Midlands anxious to take their places.

The match against All England was a great day for the Yorkshire villagers. The delvers from the quarries, the handloom weavers from their cottages, the wool combers from the water-driven mills, the shepherds, the blacksmith, the saddle maker, the wheel-wright, assembled in the village field. They brought their pints of ale from the pub and stuck them in niches in the dry stone wall. They gobbled their sandwiches in the interval. Mellowed by the sun and the ale, they cheered their heroes vociferously and heckled and tormented their enemies.

Superciliously the Internationals smiled at the cross-batted lunges of the villagers; they laughed uproariously at the incongruous, unorientated swipes of the corn miller and the potter, but, sometimes, they had laughed too soon. For Ikey and Billy would be playing for the village. Not by birth, residence or upbringing would they be entitled to do so. Nevertheless, there they were.

When the villagers went out to field, the grimaces of disdain were wiped away, the mockery and derision stifled. Aided by a splinter or two of outcropping millstone grit, belligerent Billy whistled the ball round the batsmen's skulls, or, hitting the serrated edge of a dandelion root, shot it with supersonic vehemence along the ground. Carpenter and Hayward's billycocks may have wobbled in awe, George Parr and Julius Caesar's shins tingled in dismay, but nevertheless, it was Ikey whom these master batsmen feared the most.

Year in, year out, he and Billy followed the circus round the North of England. Wherever the tourists played, the 'twins' were engaged to bowl them out, and Ikey relied not on groundsman's aid, Pennine undulation or local umpire's bias. The patriarch of Yorkshire's greatest cricketing glory, Ikey bowled slow left arm, relying on his perfect length and subtle flight. Day after day, week after week, year after year, he faced the same batsmen, the stars of their day, the select of England, yet never could they master his sublime skill. In the six seasons 1860-1865 he took 475 wickets against the tourists alone, besides playing in county matches and club matches whenever the tourists had fled to some other corner of the realm.

Poor Ikey. He died in 1867 at the early age of thirty-nine; but he had lit a beacon, a fire that was not to be quenched in a century of cricket. 'I will make thy seed as the dust of the earth', the Lord had promised Abraham. So it was to be with Ikey. Ted Peate was eleven years old, Bobby Peel ten when Ikey finally left the field. Both might have seen him, as children, when their imaginations were most vivid, at the zenith of his skill. And the line was to continue, forever unbroken, through George Hirst, Wilfred Rhodes, Roy Kilner, Hedley Verity, Arthur Booth, Johnny Wardle and Don Wilson.

Somewhere, in a Bradford graveyard, is an old, moss-encrusted stone. When I retire, like Old Mortality, with rag and cleaning spirt I will etch away the rust and mildew. And there I shall unearth the epitaph to the Father of the Flock,

  Isaac Hodgson, rest his soul,
    Could never bat but always bowl.
Through many years the tourists' skill
    Was subjugate to Ikey's will.
They took their stance with vain defiance
    Against his subtle skill and science.
Progenitor, great Almus Pater,
    Bowler divine, but batting hater.

TEST HERO WHO NEVER PLAYED

In the middle of the nineteenth century, the public school man was brought up on a diet of Classics and Divinity. Virgil, Homer, Thucydides, Aristophanes he would be able to quote in the vernacular. In the Psalms and the prophecies of Micah and Ezekiel he would be well versed. But of geography he knew nothing.

In 430 B.C. Herodotus had marked Australis vaguely in the nether regions between Oceanus Aethiopicus and Mare Erythraeum and except for convicts and kangaroos, what further knowledge was acquired? As the Reverend Arthur Ward remarked to A. G. Steel, who was sitting among the Australians at Lord's before the start of their match, 'Ah, Mr. Steel, I hear you are going to play against the niggers'.

And, of course, the 'lower orders' (as all the rest of the community was known to the cognoscenti) had no education at all.

In 1878 the first Australian touring team came to play in England. Of their 40 matches seven were played in Yorkshire against eighteens at Elland, Batley, Hunslet, Hull, Keighley, Yeadon and Scarborough.

But if the tourists thought they would be playing cricket as laid down in the M.C.C. rules against these communities, they were in for a shock.

Wherever they played, the villagers turned out in force, hoping for the downfall of the tourists. The pits closed; the looms stopped. The miners and weavers lined the field, resting their pints in the niches in the dry stone walls and exhorting their heroes to win, and whether the victory was accomplished within or without the rules of the M.C.C. mattered not one jot. Often on a wicket that would have caused Fuller Pilch to nip back into the pavilion to fetch his scythe, the rampant villagers struck alarm and awe into the hearts of the tourists.

Nor did the umpires feel it their duty to apply the laws of the game as laid down by a pack of Londoners. Without fear, but certainly not without favour, they gave their decisions.

There was in Yorkshire, at this time, a band of bowlers whose actions would not have been countenanced at Lord's. They chucked and shied and threw with a speed and abandon that terrified the Australians. But whatever the umpires' personal opinions of these deliveries might have been, they saw it neither as their duty nor their desire to penalise the villagers by denouncing their champions.

The second Australian touring team in 1880 met with the same treatment. They screamed and squirmed but to no avail. At Elland the Australian manager complained, 'Osborne shied in a manner which astonished the Australians, but far more latitude seems to be allowed to bowlers in England than in the colonies, where unfair bowling is at once put down'. And against Batley he grumbled, 'The bowling of Ackroyd was deliberate shying'. Nor was there any sympathy for the visitors. A reverend gentleman, writing of these Australians, with little milk of human kindness in his breast, had said, 'Those of us who can remember these early tours will not need to be told that in those days our visitors were shocking bad losers'.

In spite of their agony in Yorkshire the 1880 Australians had a successful tour, so much so that towards the end of the season Lord Harris persuaded W. G. Grace to arrange a match to be played against England at Kennington Oval in early September, the first time the two countries had ever met.

But before the first Test Match the Australians had to play at Scarborough. And there, waiting for them, was a gentleman of fiery outlook and fierce delivery. 'One Franks went on to bowl', says the report, 'but literally threw the ball. The Australians remonstrated against the Aunt Sally type of cricket, and the umpire threw out a caution, but all to no purpose. Bannerman, declining to play him, stood to one side and so lost his wicket; this amid unseemly jeering and rude remarks from the crowd, who evidently seemed delighted that the Australians were for once nonplussed'.

Bannerman was a master batsman, 'a most charming player, his off-side driving being magnificent', but it was not Charles Bannerman that England had to fear at the Oval.

There was, in the Australian team, the great 'Demon' Spofforth, fastest bowler in the world, who had already taken over 700 wickets on the tour at an average of about five runs each. He was the menace England would have to face at the Oval. Bannerman was there merely for One Franks to get a sight of the wicket and to bring his speed and ferocity to the boil.

As Bannerman, shaken and humiliated, thankfully departed, on to the field at Scarborough came the Mighty Spofforth. One Franks girded up his loins, gave an extra lick to his bowling fingers, thundered towards the wicket, threw the ball with all the energy and verve of which he was capable . . . and smashed Demon Spofforth's finger to pulp.

England won the Test Match at the Oval. W. G. Grace scored 152, although he had stated that he 'did not expect any conspicuous personal success'. But that was before the Scarborough match, before One Franks had settled the result of the first Test Match. 'It must be mentioned in fairness to the Australians', said the Badminton library, commenting on the game, 'that their best bowler, Spofforth, was prevented by an accident from taking part in the match'.

Accident? Sort of. But they never thought of sending for One Franks to play for Yorkshire or England, nor even, to this day, do they mention his name in the roll of cricket honour.

If you lived in the South of England you might have thought that England's champions were Dr. W. G. Grace, Lord Harris or the Honourable Ivo Bligh, but the men of Scarborough, in 1880, knew who had won the first Test Match for England at Kennington Oval.

O my Jackson and my Leyland long ago
With apologies to Francis Thompson

Right The aged Wilfred Rhodes demonstrates his bowling grip to a friend, Norman Hazell.

Centre right The 'cross-bat village greener', Maurice Leyland.

Far right Schofield Haigh, neglected equal, as a bowler, with Hirst and Rhodes.

Below far right Yorkshire champions 1908. Behind: Hardisty, Bates, Newstead, Rothery, Myers, J. Hoyland (scorer). In front Wilkinson, Haigh, Hirst, Lord Hawke, Hunter, Denton, Rhodes.

Below A Yorkshire XI with Lord Hawke (centre) as captain. Back row: D. Hunter, G. H. Hirst, C. E. M. Wilson and W. Rhodes; middle row: E. Smith, F. W. Milligan, Lord Hawke, F. S. Jackson and J. Tunnicliffe; front row: D. Denton, S. Haigh and J. T. Brown.

27

Tom Emmett, 'the greatest clown that ever walked on to a cricket field'.

THE COMIC FROM HALIFAX

Tom Emmett was born in Halifax on September 3 1841. He was the greatest clown that ever walked on to a cricket field. Yet, at a time when county cricket was ruled by the scions of the nobility, when the professional was the labourer to do the bidding of an often inferior amateur, and when the serf was left in no doubt as to who were his masters, he played for Yorkshire for 23 consecutive years. And even when he was laid off at the age of 47 there were many who thought that his career could have continued for two or three seasons more to the county's benefit.

He was of quaint appearance, rubicund of countenance, with a nose that gave the impression that his staple diet was ale. He was erratic, excitable, outspoken, reckless and often unreliable.

He was professional captain of Yorkshire for five seasons before handing over, in 1883, to the youthful Martin Hawke. They were a wayward team in those days, their fielding being so poor that it was said, 'They were too polite to run their opponents out'. Their misdemeanours in this direction were flagrant, and none suffered more from their butterfingers than Tom.

'What's the team like, Tom?' asked the Hon. M. B. Hawke, when he took up his appointment. 'Well, Mr. Hawke', said Tom, with bitter memories of their infirmities, 'there's an epidemic in this team. But don't fret yersen, sir. It isn't catching.'

Yet he had many saving graces. He was described as one of the most popular and proficient professional cricketers of his time. He was tireless, uncomplaining, merry; he could, with his cheerfulness and bonhomie, lift the heart of any struggling team that had given up the ghost; he had the gift of the blarney that assuages wrath, he was a sportsman to his fingertips and there was in him a hidden dignity which condemned anything that contrasted with his opinion of how the game should be conducted.

And, perhaps more important than any other of these endearing qualities, he could bowl the unplayable ball. He bowled fast left arm with a curious and puzzling delivery and his impossible ball would pitch between the batsman's legs and the wicket, break towards the off and just displace the bails. And all the outgoing batsman could say was that the ball would have beaten any man on earth. But between sending down his masterpieces he was grotesquely erratic. He bowled more wides than anyone else who ever went on to bowl in any class of cricket, so wide, in fact, were many of them that they were far beyond the reach of the slips.

Yet he was in no way perturbed by his own eccentricity or inaccuracy.

At the end of one of his more fearsome and unproductive spells, Lord Hawke ordered him to take his sweater, called him over and asked him severely if he knew how many wides he'd bowled already that season. 'No idea, my Lord', said the uncontrite Tom. 'Forty-five', said His Lordship in frigid tones that were meant to deflate him. Tom smiled at him serenely, 'Then I hope you'll let me go on bowling a bit longer. It'll be fifty soon and then 'appen I shall have earned mi talent brass!'

In 1878 he went with George Ulyett, another boisterous Yorkshireman, to Australia with a team of amateurs under the captaincy of Lord Harris. George and he were there to bowl out the opposition so that Lord Harris and his gentlemen friends could practise their batting. The match averages of the tour give the number of wides bowled as: 1 by V. F. Royle, 3 by A. N. Hornby, 1 by the great Lord Harris himself . . . and 33 by Tom.

But Tom took 137 wickets, more than twice as many as anybody else on the tour.

And for once he had a legitimate excuse for his waywardness. In those halcyon days cricket teams were not chosen with the thought and care that is given to sporting events today. Sport was a pleasure, not an event of world importance where, or so we are given to believe, national survival may depend on the result of a football match. So Lord Harris and his merry men spent many convivial weeks sailing to the other end of the earth, no doubt danced with the ladies and dined with the captain, and not till they had arrived and were making preparations for their first match did they realise that they had forgotten to take a wicket-keeper with them!

Tom's vocabulary and expressions were succinct and pithy, suited to the bar parlour but hardly to a lady's ear. Yet Lady Londesborough, whose husband was a

Lockwood, Peate, Ulyett and Tom Emmett, 'the comic from Halifax', making impressive pretensions to learning on a visit to Cambridge University when Lord Hawke was an undergraduate.

great patron of Yorkshire cricket, made a crony of him, and whenever the opportunity arose, would take him away for a chat.

When his fellow professionals heard her merry laugh ring out and saw her reluctance to depart they questioned Tom about his 'affair'. Tom, of course, had an answer. He allus tried to suit himself to his company, he said, and even if he did let slip a flowery thing or two, her ladyship only smiled the more affably and set him at his ease, 'and that is how we get on so well'.

One evening during the Scarborough Festival, coming across the honourable gentlemen in their toggery of white ties and tails on their way to some grand concert he had the temerity to inquire of them if they were the minstrels from the show on the pier.

But Tom was not in the Yorkshire team to provide comedy. He was there to bowl. In 1866 and again in 1867 he was top of the All England bowling averages. In 1868 he was second. In 1886, almost two decades later, he was still second.

For over twenty years he was the willing horse, the inexhaustible bowler, who, in spite of his wides and misalignment, could bowl them all out.

On his retirement he went as coach to Rugby School. He would not make silk purses out of sows' ears, but we can see him, when practice was done, sitting in some dusky corner of the pavilion surrounded by a group of admiring youths, rapturously listening to his tales and anecdotes of famous players. And he, in his inimitable way, would teach them what is far more important than the perfection of the stroke, he would teach them that geniality, comradeship, and sportsmanship rather than victory and defeat, are what cricket is really about.

THE CHAPEL-GOER

Louis Hall was a God-fearing man. When the swashbuckling beer-swillers with whom his cricket skill obliged him to associate dashed off to the nearest pub, Louis went in search of a Methodist chapel.

Thin as a lath, saturnine, heavy-moustached, of stern, ascetic appearance, Louis, both in his life and his cricket, eschewed the Devil and all his works. For him there were no pints and pork pies at the luncheon interval; no long, alcoholic inquests on the day's play in the evening; no going to the wicket in the middle of the afternoon wondering which of the several balls he could see it would be best to hit.

Nor, on the long train journeys between matches, would Louis be found playing ha'penny nap or pontoon on the corner of an upturned cricket bag. Among his cricket tackle would be found a Methodist hymn book, and probably a copy of John Wesley's sermons.

Yes, Louis was a chapel-going man. He sat, when the commitments of his travelling life allowed, at the feet of the local preachers. Intently he listened to their doctrines of the proximity of Hell, and of how, if the strait and narrow path to Paradise were to be followed, frivolity and entertainment and all such satanic works should be banished from his world.

Into his life, and to the wicket when he went in to bat, he took the doctrines of his mentors. George Ulyett might, with full red-blooded earthiness, knock the ball over the pavilion at Headingley. Billy Bates might dance down the wicket and drive three balls in succession with exquisite wrist work through the covers to the boundary. Even Lord Hawke himself might occasionally execute a somewhat stiff-armed square cut, but such levity was not for Louis. His Heaven he might have won – but he gave the bowlers Hell.

George Macaulay was once bowling to George Gunn of Nottingham at Park Avenue. Gunn was an opening batsman of genius. Beside orthodox strokes, he would, when the wayward mood was upon him, extemporise in a way that made connoisseurs cringe. Furthermore, instead of standing in his block hole, he would walk up and down the wicket as the bowler was coming in. As Gunn was perambulating, Macaulay stopped in his run-up. Angered by the perversity of this procrastination, he ordered, 'Stop boogering about, George, and stand still'.

There was never any need to tell Louis to stop 'boogering about'. Gay abandon, light-hearted enjoyment, the delights of stroke play he eschewed. With him to the wicket he took a straight and dead bat.

He began his Yorkshire career in 1873, and, for twenty years, opened the innings. There was no effulgence to his batting. Billy Bates, George Ulyett, Tom Emmett and Eph. Lockwood might swing their bats at the other end, but Louis stuck in his block hole. He prodded and poked, but there he stayed, often from the beginning of the innings to the very end. At Canterbury in 1885 it took him 70 minutes to score a run and in two and three quarter hours he made 12 not out.

One afternoon at Lord's Louis was going his sober way. A tired bowler, who, from morning, had made no impression on his passive bat, turned to Tom Emmett, who was at the other end, and said, 'I wish you'd shove a pin into Hall'.

'Nay that 'ud be no good', replied Tom. "E 'asn't enough flesh to make a pin cushion.'

On another occasion at Brighton he went on and on, batting right through the innings, scoring, in his gentle way, 124 not out.

Opposing him was Humphreys, the lob bowler. The accredited way to play lob bowling was to run down the wicket and hit. You hit a six, or a four, or were caught out on the boundary. But not Louis. Gingerly he poked the slow underhands back to Humphreys, taking only the quiet single when the opportunity was offered. In disgust Humphreys turned to a colleague. He'd be glad, he said, to pay for the coffin that would hold the remains of the Methodist Tyke.

Louis played 336 matches for Yorkshire and scored over 12,000 runs. Eight times he batted through the innings, often for small scores such as 33 against Warwickshire in 1891 and 34 against Surrey in 1888. He scored twelve centuries, his highest being 166 against the North Riding at Middlesbrough. He shared in a hundred partnerships with Ulyett, Fred Lee, Bobby Peel and Billy Bates. In 1884 and 1885 he played for the Players against the Gentlemen.

Aware of his own limitations, for 20 years he bore, on Yorkshire's behalf, the heat of the noonday sun. He was the rock at which bowlers battered in vain while his more exuberant colleagues reaped their harvest of runs at the other end.

But if his mode of life was seen as a shining example to the younger generation, his batting was not!

It can have fallen to the lot of few men of such singular worth and sterling character to have earned so much censure and been so vehemently criticised, castigated and downright insulted while doing the job to which, at least by the Yorkshire cricket committee, they had been called in their earthly span.

Louis Hall, 'a God-fearing man' who 'gave the bowlers hell', with the Yorkshire County team he captained in 1884. With him are (back row) Peate, Emmett, Turner (scorer), Harris, Hunter; (middle row) Rawlin, Lee, Peel, Ulyett; (in front) Bates, Grimshaw.

'Spy' cartoon of Lord Hawke, famous Yorkshire captain.

SUPER BOSS

Lord Hawke was a Christian and a prayerful man. When he was first taking his teams on overseas tours and he found out that matches were sometimes played on a Sunday his moral convictions were shattered. In his agony he sought religious guidance and a clerical buddy gave him what amounted to a heavenly dispensation – provided he attended matins before play began.

So, in India, America, Argentina, South Africa, Australia or wherever his cricketing perambulations took him, he invited his team to accompany him to morning service. And since an 'invitation' from Lord Hawke was tantamount to 'volunteering' in H.M. Forces, his team would on Sundays enter the cathedral, church, chapel, synagogue or temple nearest the ground – in line of seniority, I suppose, with amateurs, of course, in the lead.

Alas, in later years, after a lifetime of service to cricket, his addiction to speaking to God brought him opprobrium from the Great British Public. For he prayed that no professional should ever captain England, and, thereafter, was consigned to eternal damnation by those enlightened in the modern outlook that all men are, or should be, equal.

As a boy he had more inherent cricket potential than any man ever born. Throughout his life he played billiards left-handed and shot from the left shoulder. When, as a little boy at his prep school he attended his first net, he naturally took up a left-handed stance. Shocked, the hidebound coach explained that while some professional cricketers and village bumpkins might stand that way, young gentlemen did not. Thereupon he turned the child round and insisted that he should bat right-handed.

And so Martin Hawke did throughout his career. He captained Yorkshire, he played for the Gentlemen against the Players, he scored his centuries in first class cricket. And all the time batting the wrong way round. Would even Len Hutton, batting left-handed, or Gary Sobers, batting right-handed, with all their skill and ability, have scored hundreds against Lindwall, Miller, Statham, Trueman and Laker?

Lord Hawke captained Yorkshire for 28 years and was president for 41 years, these offices overlapping from 1898 to 1910. Never had a man such pride in the county. Unlike all other counties, Yorkshire allows none born outside its boundaries to defend the White Rose with bat or ball. Only three men throughout the county cricket club's existence have broken this rule: Cecil Parkin, W. G. Keighley and Lord Hawke himself.

Cecil Parkin was born withing spitting distance of the border. In 1906 he played one innings, scoring 0, and took two wickets for 25 runs before it was discovered, in horror, that his birthplace was Durham! Unsung, he was allowed to depart to Lancashire, where he attained international fame. W. G. Keighley, born in France of good Yorkshire stock, was allowed to play between 1947 and 1951, it being argued in his favour that a continental birthplace did not make him available for any other county and therefore disbar him from Yorkshire.

And the third off-comer was, of course, Lord Hawke himself, born near Gainsborough in Lincolnshire, where his father was a country rector.

In 1883 he took over from Tom Emmett a team which he later described as consisting of 'Louis Hall and ten ale-cans'. To them he brought discipline and pride and, when he felt the occasion demanded it, the high-handed authority of the martinet.

Ted Peate and Bobby Peel he dismissed from the team at the height of their international fame for minor misdemeanours and, in 1899, at Lord's, sacked Bobby Moorhouse for failing to make an effort to take a catch in the outfield. When asked about it, Moorhouse replied that he didn't think it was coming so far, 'and when Ah seed it up theer Ah said, "Oh, damn it"'. Angrily, Lord Hawke retorted that if he wouldn't try, he'd have to go, and that was the end of Bobby Moorhouse's county cricket.

Nothing pleased his lordship better than to score runs, but his ability did not normally entitle him to a high place in the batting order of a team so powerful as Yorkshire.

In May 1896 Yorkshire scored 887 against Warwickshire without declaring. It is the highest total ever scored in a county match. It left Yorkshire no time to dismiss Warwickshire twice and occupied 274 overs. What was the object of such a useless record? Well, seven wickets had fallen for 448 when Lord Hawke came in at number nine. Santall (65 overs; 2 wickets for 223), Ward (62 overs; 2 wickets for 175), Glover (30 overs; 1 wicket for 154) and Pallett (75 overs; 4 wickets for 184) were already tiring. Here was the opportunity for some fun. Lord Hawke scored another 166 runs and with Bobby Peel (210 not out) carried the score to 740. His lordship hugely enjoyed his slaughter of the weary bowlers and when he was out at last, bowled by the persevering Pallett, decided to give George Hirst an innings. He had been waiting long enough at number ten. So George went in and plundered another 85 runs. And after the innings Lord Hawke had the temerity to ask for the ball as a souvenir!

His plans did not always go so well. In 1898 at Chesterfield against Derbyshire he thought he would like an innings. So, irrespective of merit, he put himself in at number three after Brown and Tunnicliffe and went to put his pads on.

He did not expect to have to wait long. Poor 'Long John' Tunnicliffe had had a series of misfortunes on his way to the ground. He had had nothing to eat since teatime the day before. He had booked in at a dirty inn, found the bed clothes damp and sat up all night in a chair. Obviously, he was in no state to bat long. But Brown and Tunnicliffe scored 554 for the first wicket and it was twelve o'clock on the second day before Lord Hawke got his innings.

It was a natural progression for one of so strong a character to become chairman of England's Test Selection Committee. But here his lordship was torn between two desires. Much as he wanted England to win the Tests, he wanted Yorkshire to win the County Championship even more, and he had built up such a powerful team in Yorkshire that England wanted its players.

For the Test Match at Manchester in 1902 England automatically chose George Hirst, Wilfred Rhodes and Stanley Jackson and then wanted to include, among the thirteen, Schofield Haigh as off-spin bowler. Now Schofie was the best off-spin bowler in England as well as a powerful middle order hitter, but Lord Hawke feared that he would be left drumming his heels as number twelve while Yorkshire were missing his services, so he objected. Fred Tate, of lesser ability, was therefore substituted and Schofie returned to his county duties.

Fred Tate played, missed a vital catch and, going in last when England wanted eight to win, was bowled out with England only four short of victory. After the

Below left *'His lengthy lordship of Hawke.'* **Right** Lord Hawke (batting *'the wrong way round'*)

match malicious tongues were heard to say that Lord Hawke lost more Test Matches for England than anyone else who had never played.

He was adept at winning the toss, particularly on his tours to far flung parts of the British Empire. But it was not all pure luck. He would hand a golden sovereign to his opposing captain, invite him to toss, and, when the coin was in the air, call, 'It's a woman'. And, of course, when it came down with Queen Victoria's head on one side and Britannia on the other, it was! Whichever side was uppermost Lord Hawke would look at it with satisfaction and say, 'We'll bat'.

Another record of which he was proud was that he was the offspring of one of the earliest of all courtships. The first time his father saw his mother was the day he, as a county parson, baptized her when she was a babe in arms.

But he was happiest taking his teams to all parts of the world. Between 1887 and 1912 he toured Australia, India, Canada, the United States, South Africa, the West Indies and Argentina.

In 1889, when thoughts of the Mutiny were still fresh in the minds of the natives, he played at Lucknow. He might have scored a century and demonstrated the superiority of the white raj, but his 'duck' was a stroke of pure genius, probably doing more to cement Anglo-Indian friendship than all the machinations of Foreign Secretaries and Viceroys.

In 1885 in South Africa, he went to gaol to play poker with those condemned to death for the Jameson Raid. His visit was supposed to be an attempt to cheer the prisoners up . . . but he won £98 off them. No doubt they could afford it. They paid Kruger £25,000 for their release.

But his greatest moments were in the United States where he and his men arrived almost as beings from another planet bringing with them some newly concocted ball game.

Rapturously they were met at Philadelphia. 'Quaker City Society bows before the English Gentlemen' said one headline, and a war correspondent began his account of the first battle.

'Through lorgnettes, field glasses, monocles and whatnots, Philadelphia society saw today a real game of cricket played . . . Cricket is English from beginning to end – if it has any end. Consequently society turned out *en masse* today and camped round the big field at Mannheim on coaches, drays, breaks, T-carts and tandems.

'"My, ain't they big fellows", said a Germantown girl, critically overhauling them with a pair of opera glasses. She was right. They looked almost elephantine as they strolled across the field in their white toggery. Then a queer little chap, wearing a white hat and a red nose, set up three little sticks in one place and three little sticks in another. This was all that there was to it.'

With the gentle elegance that was the hallmark of bygone cricket the game continued its amiable course. Whenever an Englishman was out the band struck up 'God Save the Queen'.

But, at last, the moment that all had waited for arrived. The correspondent continued, 'Another tall figure came meandering across the field in a sort of shambling walk – and no wonder. His legs were fitted with a couple of circular washboards and his hands were mailed with lengthy gauntlets. He looked for all the world like Buck Taylor, the King of the Cowboys. For a few minutes his lengthy lordship of Hawke was the bull's-eye for ten thousand pairs of eyes. They did not seem to worry him any. He ranted from wicket to wicket. A wicked ball bounded up and hit Lord Hawke an awful whack on the gauntleted knuckles. Society groaned. His lordship merely put his hand behind his back, tweedled his fingers, looked up at the sky placidly without an audible word. Who can doubt, however, that he talked Parsee to himself?'

The same adulation was not given to the home team. Of one of the Philadelphians a journalist wrote, 'All the morning an imposing individual with a sky-blue coat, a white braided cap, a pair of grey side whiskers and an air of importance had been walking around the ground telling what he knew about cricket. People were appalled at his thorough insight into the game. Out from the club-house he floated, a symphony in blue. What a walk he had. It was a cross between that of Henry Irving and a straddle-bug. It was style though, clear through. He looked at the sky as though to select a favourable cloud to knock the ball over; then he balanced his bat in his hands and pranced along, just as de Wolf Hopper does after a third encore. "That's the boy for Nellie", said somebody. He stepped in front of the wicket, struck an attitude like a petrified Adonis and looked at the unhappy bowler with an eagle eye.

'"He is good for a six, anyway. I can tell it by his looks", murmured a dude in the grand stand.

'"How handsome he is", whispered a young society woman to her escort, "I'll wager he makes a hundred".

'The bowler was not alarmed. He stepped back a few paces, ran forward, whirled his arm like a cartwheel and let the ball travel. The symphony in blue did not have time to realise that he was alive; he had an awfully pretty bat in his hands too, but the ball whisked by his classic shins. There was a dull explosion at the wickets, and, as far as cricket was concerned, the symphony was dead. He smiled a sort of sickly smile, said "Baw Jawve", below his breath and crawled back.'

They played at Philadelphia, Boston, New York and Massachusetts. There were balls and banquets in their honour. Charming partners devoted themselves to teaching the tourists a new waltz step.

'Lord Hawke', wrote a correspondent, 'has already made a great impression, and, as he is a comparatively young bachelor, it is a safe prediction that some of the golden girls of the metropolis will find him too nice for anything.'

The tourists did not win back an empire, but perhaps they did more; they captured the hearts of every girl in the Eastern States.

More than one young Yankee had his nose put out by the gay and glamorous Englishmen, and was glad to see the back of them. 'Beefy, solemn-looking men, a more depressingly clad company it would be hard to find', whined one. But perhaps his girl had given her heart to one of the Englishmen who, at Philadelphia after the match, had drunk sixty-four toasts and was still on his feet at the end of it.

It could only be mental aberration that prevented the Prime Minister from sending Lord Hawke to Washington as ambassador. He had a habit of always getting his own way. There is little doubt he would have made cricket America's national game, caused the Declaration of Independence to be revoked and returned the States to their rightful home in the Empire.

Ted Peate, master of length and flight.

THE PERFECT BOWLER

In spite of the fame which Wilfred Rhodes, George Hirst, Hedley Verity and Bobby Peel accumulated, it is probable that Ted Peate was the greatest left-arm bowler who ever played for Yorkshire. Perhaps he was the greatest who ever lived. Certainly he got his wickets at a cheaper rate than any of his successors. For while Rhodes's cost him 16 runs each, Peel's 15, Hirst's 18 and Verity's nearly 14, Ted got his at 12½ each.

His life and career with Yorkshire were all too short. He was only forty-four when he died in 1900, and his career with the county ended in 1887 after eight years of unbroken success.

Suddenly there was oblivion. By 1887 he had gone, vanished from the game, finished, discarded – at an age when, by modern standards, a slow bowler has hardly completed his apprenticeship.

'Failing eyesight compelled his retirement', wrote a reverend gentleman, but ... in those days few Yorkshire pros were averse to wetting their whistles, nor did they lack admirers always ready to thrust another pint in front of them. Often a packet of sandwiches in a corner of the ale tent had to suffice for a meal.

A hot day in the sun, the weariness of the flesh, the comfort of the best armchair, sycophantic company and just one more bottle took the last wicket of more than one Victorian cricketer.

'Long John' Tunnicliffe wrote to Lord Hawke long after one of these occasions. It was at Lord's. Yorkshire were all out by four and old Billy Barnes, nearing the end of his great career, retired to refresh himself. But MCC wickets fell quickly and Barnes, unexpectedly, was called from the beer tent to bat before the close of play. John couldn't be certain whether Barnes was sober or not, but as he slouched to the wicket, he remarked with a wink that he could see several balls knocking about and he thought it would be safest to go for the middle one!

'Long John' feared that Billy's career might end in ruins, but what could have been a tragedy proved instead a triumph. Barnes scored about 80, and his strokes on the off-side were masterly. Tunnicliffe well knew that if Lord Hawke had detected the truth it would have meant disaster for Billy.

'One of my saddest tasks was to dismiss Ted Peate from the Yorkshire team', said Lord Hawke. And so it must have been. For when his Lordship was an undergraduate at Cambridge it was one of his pleasures and idiosyncracies to entertain Peate to breakfast in his rooms when Yorkshire were playing the University. And Ted and his friends, George Ulyett and Tom Emmett, whose schoolings had probably ended by their tenth year, would proceed to adorn themselves in gowns and mortar boards, to take down learned tomes from the bookcases and pose for their photographs; photographs which, if they had come before the eyes of the University authorities, might have led to his lordship suffering a period of rustication, if not dismissal, from his seat of learning.

Ted, alas, like many another of the old Yorkshire cricketers, 'had too many friends'. It was glasses that presaged his downfall, but not the kind the reverend gentleman had in mind.

He was pot-bellied, and, said a contemporary, 'to look at him you would have thought he was the last man to have deputised in a troop of Clown Cricketers'. He fielded with less than gay abandon, and batted because the laws of the game insisted that he must do.

But his rotundity and gaumlessness disappeared when he went on to bowl. 'He was blessed with the most perfect action of any man I have seen deliver the ball', wrote one of his admirers.

In his youth Peate had been a wild, riproaring fast bowler, but in 1879, at the age of 23, when he joined the Yorkshire team, he had developed into slow left arm. He suffered from no inhibitions, he was cursed by no theories and was fortunate to play before the age when science and coaching have hung a millstone of abnegation and timidity around the ambition and natural talent of the young.

A master of length and flight, he could pitch and float the ball to his whim, luring the adventurous to catastrophe, blandly coercing the hesitant and timorous to their doom.

Immediately he took his place among the leading bowlers in the land. Ninth in the first class bowling averages in 1879, fifth in 1880, by 1881 he was the leading wicket taker in England, and, in 1882, with 214 wickets he had almost 100 more than his nearest rival. So it continued – 120 in 1883, 137 in 1884, 115 in 1885.

And that, practically, was the end of Ted's career. Throughout this time he had kept Bobby Peel in the second team. As soon as Ted was dismissed, Peel became an England bowler. He could also score 1,000 runs a year. He was less than a year younger than Peate, but, with all his skill, which many said was equal to Wilfred Rhodes's, Peel had to play second fiddle to Peate while he was available.

Of batsmen Peate feared none, disdained none, probably respected none, but, if he had to throw down a challenge, then, only before the very best would he deign to cast his gage.

In those days W. G. Grace was the scourge of the country, a Goliath of power, flaunting his mastery proudly as ever did the champion of Gath over the Valley of Elah. His challenge was there for anyone who dared to accept.

Thoughtfully Peate took it up.

This was in the halcyon days before we were bedevilled with new ball theories. Scarlet or mud-caked, glossy or battered, a cricket ball was a cricket ball. Peate took it at the start of the match, trusted to his good left arm, tossed it gently towards the Doctor's bat, and –

| 1879 Bowled Peate 13 | 1881 Bowled Peate 8 | 1882 Bowled Peate 0 |
| 1885 Bowled Peate 1 | 1886 Bowled Peate 9 | |

were some of Grace's innings against Yorkshire.

The Doctor suffered neither fools nor masters gladly. The thirst for revenge had bitten deep into his soul. In 1887, when Peate did not play, his four innings against Yorkshire were, 183 not out, 97, 92 and 20.

Throughout his short career Peate was an England international player. His most famous performance was at Holbeck in 1883 against Surrey. On a dead wicket Yorkshire only just managed to score 100, but, in reply, Peate took eight wickets for five runs to dismiss Surrey for 31.

His most notorious was at the Oval in 1882 in the Test Match against Australia.

He had already taken 8 wickets for 71 runs, but on the evening of the last day England wanted 9 runs to win when he went in to bat at number eleven. And the reason that he was number eleven was that a cricket team only contained eleven players. Had it contained twelve he would certainly have been number twelve.

At the other end was Charley Studd, a famous amateur batsman of the day, and in those days English cricket was ruled by the blue blood of Olde England.

Around Ted in the pavilion had gathered the pundits, the theorists the advisers, the selectors and the committee. And, in different words, their advice was all the same, 'Keep your wicket up. Stay there. Block it. Leave the runs to Charley'.

Philosophically, weighing this plethora of advice, Ted wandered down the pavilion steps and out into the middle. He took a mighty heave at the ball, missed it and saw his wickets scattered.

Around him, on his return, like vultures gathered the aristocracy of England, demanding, in threatening tones, the why and wherefore of his transgression.

But Ted was a true Tyke. He was not to be browbeaten by this onslaught from his 'betters'. Quietly he shrugged his shoulders. 'Aye, well', he said slowly, 'it were like this. Ah were all reyt aht theer missen. But Ah couldn't trust Mister Studd at t'other end.'

He would not show them his anguish, but later, when he was sitting miserable and alone in the dressing room a friend asked him what he had been thinking about out there at the wicket. Sadly he confessed, 'Ah were thinkin' hah they'd all say, "Good owd Ted", when it went sailin' ovver t'pavilion'.

It was a measure of his greatness, that, even after all this, they still picked him to play for England.

W. G. Grace (from a painting by J. E. Brewn) fell like Goliath to Ted Peate's David.

George Hirst (left) and Wilfred Rhodes. In 1902 at Birmingham they bowled Australia out for 36.

THE GREATEST COUNTY CRICKETER OF ALL TIME

In September 1951, on the occasion of his eightieth birthday, I was invited by a North Country magazine to write an appreciation of George Hirst's cricket career.

I made an appointment to see him, but when I arrived at his little terrace house in Huddersfield, those who were looking after him and his wife took me aside before I met him. 'You'll have to make allowances for him', they apologised. 'He doesn't remember much.'

When we had shaken hands, George inquired in a yonderly but polite way, 'Did you ever see me laik cricket?'

'Yes, once', I said, 'when I was a little lad.' 'And did I do owt?' he asked. 'I don't know', I admitted. 'All I can remember is that there were chaps going round t'field with trays hawking "George Hirst Toffee".'

His eyes lit up. 'By gum', he smiled, 'it were good toffee!'

Perhaps we had established a common bond. There were other things in life more interesting to an old man than this interminable talk of bygone cricket days. He told of his early life in his native Kirkheaton, neighbour to that mighty cricket nursery, Lascelles Hall. When he was ten years old he had gone to work as a wirer – a sort of equivalent to a textile twister's reacher-in – to a handloom weaver. 'But I didn't stop with him long', George admitted. 'He'd no interest in cricket. He spent all his brass backing hosses.'

For a year or two he was a cattle drover before, in his teens, making his way to the verge of the county cricket team.

Before he was established he talked of being engaged for a week to play at Honley Feast. He could travel daily from his home but another county player, who lived in the Sheffield area, had to put up for the week at the village pub.

'And every morning when I got there at about eleven o'clock the landlord would shout out, "George, come in here for a minute, lad. He's fast asleep and drunk as a lord on t'top of t'billiard table". T'match started at half-past eleven, but we squirted a whole soda water syphon in his face, donned him in his cricket flannels, and got him onto t'field in time to start. And nobody but me and t'landlord ever knew t'state he'd been in half an hour before.'

Gently I led him to his prodigious feats with the county team but until something unexpected was introduced, the recollection seemed of little consequence.

'In 1905', I said, 'you made the highest total ever scored for Yorkshire in county cricket.' He nodded in agreement.

'Three hundred and forty-one against Leicestershire', I went on.

He looked up, slightly surprised. 'Was it so many?'

'Yes', I said, 'and they reckoned you ought to have been given out leg before wicket before you'd broken your duck.'

He chortled with fun. 'I remember', he laughed. 'I were reyt in t'front but t'umpire gave me not out.'

No man ever earned or deserved more eulogies. 'The greatest county cricketer who ever lived', Lord Hawke wrote of him in 1924. In 1903 it was said that 'by universal consent he was the greatest all-round cricketer in the world' and that, 'he is as strong as a lion and a glutton for work'. And after his death, the son of one of his contemporaries in the team called him 'the kindest and most generous man I have ever known.'

The story is told that when George and two of his county team mates from Huddersfield arrived at the station on their way home from a match, they always went to the bar and George ordered, 'Three pints'. When they had supped off, number two, in his turn, said, 'Same ageean', and after this, number three, and always the same number three, pulled out his watch and said, 'It's time we were makin' us way hooam'.

It was also said of George that 'he would show anybody owt', and of a contemporary that he also 'would show anybody owt . . . for half a crown'.

George was a great Yorkshireman and regarded playing cricket for his county as the greatest honour that could be bestowed on him, but, unlike Wilfred Rhodes who gloried in the challenge, he never liked Test Matches, never wanted to play in them, and, except on rare occasions, did not justify himself in them.

Two Test matches stand out. In 1902 at Birmingham, Hirst and Rhodes bowled Australia out for 36. Straight after the match the Australians came to play Yorkshire at Headingley on June 2nd, 'Peace Rejoicing Day', and were bowled out by Hirst and Stanley Jackson for 23.

At the Oval in 1902 England followed on 141 behind Australia and required 263 to win in the second innings. After they had lost their first four wickets for 16 runs Gilbert Jessop thundered a mighty 104. Immaculate Stanley Jackson made 49 and when Wilfred Rhodes, the last man, came in to join Hirst 15 were still wanted.

This was the famous occasion when they were supposed to have confabulated in the middle and decided to 'get 'em in ones'. And get them they did; Hirst 58 not out, Rhodes 6 not out. And so highly was this performance rated that a collection was taken up at the Stock Exchange and Rhodes and Hirst were each presented with 'a handsome purse'.

We will not dwell too long on statistics; he would not have wanted us to do so, but . . . he played for Yorkshire for thirty years. Fourteen times he performed the cricketer's double of scoring 1,000 runs and taking 100 wickets in a season and once, incredibly, in 1906, he scored 2,000 runs and took 200 wickets, and always, after being established, he was Lord Hawke's trusted advisor.

He spoke true Yorkshire dialect. Once a silver tobacco jar was offered to the player who could tell the best story in Yorkshire dialect, and Canon E. S. Carter was to be the judge. Canon Carter was an incorrigible Yorkshire cricket enthusiast and a 'character', who allowed his ecclesiastical duties to interfere as little as possible with his cricket. Often, when he was batting and it was time for evensong, he would drop his bat on the pitch, hurry away to take the service, return as quickly as possible and resume his innings. Also at Yorkshire cricket gatherings, without much pressure or alcohol being applied, he sang, 'Where is another sweet as myself?' and 'Norah, darling', and he is reputed, one Sunday morning, after having made a good score on the Saturday, to have declared on the conclusion of the first

Bible reading, 'Here endeth the first innings'. So, this rabid Yorkshireman judged the contest and had no hesitation in presenting the tobacco jar to George.

George was the discoverer and instigator of swing bowling. With a new ball he could make his fast medium left arm deliveries veer in enormously from the off. Before his day, bowlers used to rub the ball on the ground to erase the polish. It was a skill he attributed to his short, stumpy fingers. A Huddersfield professional once asked him to show him how to swerve the ball. 'Let's look at thy hand', George said, and immediately added, 'Thou'll nivver swerve a ball with fingers like that'. 'They were like talons', George said when telling the tale.

After thirty years unstinting service, weighed down with honour and praise, he might have considered that his cricket career was over. It was really only at its threshold.

First at Eton, then with Yorkshire, he became the greatest cricket coach of all time. It was to him a duty and a pleasure combined, to which he brought his love of the game, his unflagging enthusiasm and unfailing kindness to every tyro who appeared before him

It was a kindness which never failed to find merit in even the most unworthy performances. A young man batting at the nets suffered a torrid ten minutes against a fast bowler who was later to play for England. 'Well batted, Reggie', said George when the youth was taking off his pads. 'Oh, no, Mr. Hirst', expostulated the batsman, 'I never touched one of them'. 'No', agreed, George, 'but you didn't run away from them either'.

Always his coaching was salted with a touch of impish humour. Once, when he was about sixty years of age and Yorkshire were scraping the barrel, I was batting at the nets. He watched for a few balls. Apparently my attempted cover drive didn't please him. He came down the wicket, took the bat from me and demonstrated where I should put my left foot and how I should swing into the stroke.

He returned my bat. 'Do it like that, lad', he advised. 'I'll bowl you one or two for practice.'

At a brisk medium pace he dropped them on the half volley just outside the off stump.

Doing as I was bid I sent the balls whistling into the side netting. Along came the next ball, apparently just the same. Again I swung confidently but, suddenly, the ball dipped and rattled against my pads. He put his hands on his hips and laughed down the wicket at me. 'That's t'way I used to get 'em leg before when I was laiking!'

Today half the schoolmasters and youth leaders in England have certificates and diplomas for cricket coaching. There were no such qualifications in George's day, but he had his fundamentals, his verities clear enough. He could teach only some of his pupils to play; he could, and did, teach them all to love cricket.

It was nearing tea time and I stood up to go. We shook hands and he smiled at me. 'It were champion toffee, tha knows', he said, and as I opened the door, Mrs. Hirst added, 'I wish we had four ounce of it today'.

HERO OF MAFEKING

Frank Milligan played his last game for Yorkshire in 1898. Tall, sandy-haired, straight as a guardsman, a Corinthian in outlook, a hero who might have walked straight out of the pages of *Tom Brown's Schooldays*, he was that rare person that, with all its later glories, Yorkshire cricket was never to produce again – the gay cavalier, the debonair sportsman, the carefree amateur, to whom the fruits of victory meant nothing compared with the joy of the contest.

A scion of the nobility, on leaving Eton he was sent by his father, Colonel Milligan, to live at Royds Hall and to learn the business of becoming an ironmaster at Low Moor Ironworks, of which the colonel was a director.

The story of Low Moor Ironworks had started over one hundred years before with a spendthrift county squire, a parson given to chemical experiments and a wealthy business man addicted to financial gambles.

The Corinthian buck squandered his patrimony on horses, cock-fighting mains and barefisted mills. The parson, walking over the squire's estates, kicked a brown stone and found it rich in iron ore. The financier staked his fortune on buying the squire's estate and building plant to smelt the ironstone. Thus, Low Moor Ironworks began to produce the most ductile wrought iron in the world.

When Frank Milligan joined it, Low Moor was famous for its wrought iron. No ironworks in the world could compare with it for the purity of its products. At a great industrial fair in the United States the ironmasters of Europe and America had vied with each other in the magnificence of their trade stands, in the profusion of the complicated machinery they could manufacture and in the hosts of quick talk salesmen they had assembled to boast about and advertise their products.

Low Moor sent just one man, carrying in his pocket a one-inch cube of their wrought iron. He took it to a wire drawing mill, produced mile after mile of wire, spun fine as a spider's thread, and challenged his rivals to do likewise. His challenge was unaccepted and when he returned home, Low Moor's fame was greater than ever.

So Low Moor was at the zenith of its power, but its directors, obsessed with its fame and standing, refused to move with the times. Gradually, in the field of steel production, more sophisticated furnaces were evolved; gradually, the skill of muscle and eye of the iron puddlers was being replaced by an advancing era of science, but Low Moor stood still. The admonitions of Frank and his young colleagues were ignored, their appraisals and suggestions pigeon-holed. Disillusioned, Frank gave less of his interest to the ironworks and more to the Low Moor Cricket Club which played in the lovely ground of Royds Hall where he lived.

Soon he was the most famous cricketer in the Bradford and Spen Valley areas. Batting, bowling and fielding he was a joy to watch, and he became a hero and pattern to all the youngsters in the district. To his credit still stands one of the biggest hits in all cricket history. Playing at the Dewsbury and Savile ground against Spen in a Heavy Woollen Cup final he drove a ball from Ben Hirst (a famous Cleckheaton bowler of the early 1890s) straight out of the ground and over a street, and pitched it at the feet of the local policeman patrolling his beat.

He was rarely heard to complain, but about one thing in club cricket he became thoroughly annoyed. Such an attraction was he at visiting fields that weeks in advance clubs would write to him to make sure that he would be playing so that they could 'bill' him and boost their gates.

Those were the days when each club provided its own umpire, who was often as useful a member of the team as any of the other eleven. Milligan was the great danger, and, having persuaded him to play, the next object of the twelve homers was to get him back to the pavilion. Throwing his bat into the corner of the dressing room one Saturday after a particularly disgusting decision, he complained bitterly about clubs which pestered him for weeks to play against them and then, when he'd almost knocked the ball out of the field, gave him out L.B.W.

Youthful, exuberant, he was not always, of course, successful. There were sagacious, hard-bitten professionals playing in the village teams in those days. One was the famous 'Shoey' Harrison, ex-county fast bowler, whose speed was only equalled by the flamboyance of his tongue. Once he was severely reprimanded by Lord Hawke for having remarked to the Revd. Vernon Royle (on bowling him out in a Roses match at Old Trafford) *'That's* dahned thi . . . pulpit'. And precisely how many adjectives Shoey introduced between 'thi' and 'pulpit' was a matter of argument for years by those who played in the match.

One holiday Monday Low Moor were to play Bowling Old Lane for whom Shoey was professional. Milligan, deciding he needed some practice (and, possibly, with an eye on the Bowling Old Lane fixture the following day), engaged Shoey to bowl at him on the day before. Harrison obliged, bowling all day long, and both were well satisfied with their day's work; Shoey with his handsome fee, and Milligan with his excellent practice against the enemy's demon.

Sad to say, on the Monday, Harrison, grinning maliciously, shattered Milligan's wicket with his first ball. On the Sunday he had kept back his speciality, and had learned more about Milligan's frailties than Frank had learned about Shoey's skills.

We know that as Milligan passed him on his way back to the pavilion, Harrison muttered some witticism which brought a smile to Milligan's face, but whether it was, *'That's* knocked a hoil i' thi flamin' blast furnace', has never been established.

In 1894, dispirited by the moribundity of the ironworks, he threw in his lot with the Yorkshire County team, and spent four joyous years touring the country, hitting boundaries, taking wickets, enjoying every minute of the livelong day. A more cheerful sportsman, said Lord Hawke, had never played for Yorkshire.

Alas, there were to be only four seasons for Frank Milligan. The one call that was greater than that of the Yorkshire county, the call of Queen and Country, took him to South Africa to fight in the Boer War.

In May 1902, at the close of play at Park Avenue, Bradford, the Yorkshire and Kent county cricket teams assembled at Harold Park, Low Moor, and stood bareheaded while a memorial sundial was unveiled. *To the memory of Lieut. Frank Milligan of Royds Hall, and a member of the Yorkshire County Cricket XI. He fell bravely defending the position assigned to him under Col. Plumer with the Rhodesian Frontier Forces in the attempted relief of Mafeking.*

Today it is neglected, ignored. The clock face has gone; the gnomen has been torn off; the inscription is covered with verdigris.

But at least in one place his memory is still revered. Half a mile away in St. Mark's Church, shining like gold near the organ, is a plaque bearing the inscription, *To the Glory of God and in affectionate remembrance of Lt. Frank Milligan, who was killed near Mafeking, March 31st, 1900, this tablet is erected by the Yorkshire cricket team.*

He had only four seasons with the county. He played his last game when he was twenty-eight years old. Would he, if war had spared him, have written his name on Test Match cricket like his bosom friend Stanley Jackson? Probably not. He was too carefree, too impetuous, too easy to lull to destruction by the insidious trickery of some cunning old professional bowler.

He left behind no records; just a memory of a happy, joyous life cut off before it had reached its prime, an echo of youthful laughter at the wicket.

THE GOVERNOR OF BENGAL

One August 11th, S. M. J. Woods, the Somerset captain, turned up at Headingley with a collection of gentlemen farmers dressed in deerstalkers and knickerbockers. Lord Hawke glared at them in disapproval.

Frostily he demanded to know their origin, remarking damningly that he didn't recognize one of them.

Airily, Sammy Woods told his lordship not to worry. His chaps might be as useless as they looked as cricketers 'but they're all dam' good shots', and they'd all brought their guns. It only required Lord Hawke to beat them in one day and the next day would be clear for the grouse shooting on the moors above Bolton Abbey.

On another occasion a team of southern amateurs arrived to play Yorkshire. Quickly they were polished off, Yorkshire winning by an innings and a few hundred runs. One of the opponents approached a Yorkshire professional who had been much concerned with their humiliation.

'You might have treated us more gently and made a game of it', he remonstrated. The professional gaped at him in astonishment.

'We don't laik cricket for fun i' Yorkshire', he told the Old Etonian severely.

The amateur has rarely been the glory of Yorkshire cricket. But one Yorkshire amateur, Stanley Jackson, was one of the greatest all-round cricketers who ever lived. He captained Harrow School, he captained Cambridge University, he captained England. But even this outstanding ability did not completely reconcile him to the Yorkshire professionals.

'T'trouble wi' Mr. Jackson was', one of them complained, 'you couldn't persuade him to give his undivided attention to cricket. He used to interest himself in business and politics, and once,' and here was the most heinous crime and let-down of all, 'he even went off to South Africa for a couple of seasons to fight in t'Boer War.'

The Hon. Francis (later Sir) Stanley Jackson, younger son of the first Lord Allerton of Chapel Allerton, Leeds, was born in 1870 and long before he became their scourge in 1905 the Australians knew much of his ability. In 1893, while still an undergraduate of Trinity College, he had played in his first Test Match against them and hammered their bowling to the tune of 91 runs. In 1902, in a match at Leeds, he and George Hirst had taken five wickets each in bowling out the Australians for 23.

But twice, in 1899, and 1902, Stanley Jackson had been passed over for the captaincy of England in favour of Archie Maclaren of Lancashire, and England lost both series of Test Matches. It was unfortunate, perhaps, that Jackson did not figure in the public eye as a captain, as did Maclaren. Lord Hawke was at that time captain of Yorkshire, entrenched as firmly on his throne, and, it appeared, for as long a reign as was Queen Victoria on hers.

There was no bitterness in Jackson about this slight. He played in the Tests, took part with Tom Hayward in a double-century opening stand at the Oval in 1899, and in 1902 was one of England's leading bowlers.

51

A spy cartoon of the Hon. F. S. Jackson, who allowed a mere war to interfere with his cricket!

But 1905 was Jackson's year. He had had to wait a long time for the captaincy, for in 1903-4 when at last he was asked to take the England team to Australia, he had to refuse for business reasons. But everyone knew who was to be England's captain in 1905, and Jackson had a self-confidence and determination equal to Winston Churchill's when a reluctant nation gave him at last the job for which he was born.

Jackson believed in showing his opponents his mettle at the earliest opportunity. Before the Test series began he captained the MCC against the Australians at Lord's, won the toss and scored 85 runs.

And when the Tests came along he won the toss in all five matches, won the series without losing a match, scored 144 not out against them at Leeds, 113 at Manchester, 82 not out at Nottingham and 76 at the Oval. He took five wickets for 52 runs in the first innings at Nottingham, and four wickets for 50 runs in the first innings at Lord's. He headed the batting with an average of over 70 runs per innings, in front of such stalwarts as Fry, Tyldesley, Spooner, Maclaren and Hayward. He headed the bowling averages at just over 15 runs a wicket, with George Hirst, Wilfred Rhodes and Schofield Haigh behind him.

Enough punishment, it seemed, for the Australians for one season. But, by September, perhaps the salt in the wound had dissolved. So, at the end of their tour, he captained C. I. Thornton's Eleven against them at Scarborough, again won the toss, and thrashed them to the tune of 123 runs.

But cricket was not a way of life to Stanley Jackson; it was merely a pastime. He went out to fight in the South African War as a captain in the 3rd Royal Lancashire Regiment, and, just to keep his name before the public, because his day was still to come, returned to recuperate from an illness, made a solitary appearance for the Gentlemen against the Players at Scarborough and scored 134 runs.

He was a B.A. of Trinity College, Cambridge, and an Hon. D. Litt. of both Calcutta and Dacca Universities, an Hon. LL.D. of Sheffield University, a Knight of Grace of St. John of Jerusalem and Unionist M.P. for the Howdenshire Division of Yorkshire from 1915 to 1926. He raised and commanded the 2/7 West Yorkshire Regiment in the 1914-1918 War. In 1922-1923 he was Financial Secretary to the War Office, and from 1927 to 1932 Governor of Bengal.

Was there no Achilles heel to this paragon? Oh, yes, several. He had inordinate respect for his own ability. He set his field with immense care, and whenever he bowled a ball that he felt did not reach the immaculate standard he expected of himself he would stop the game while he apologised to his captain for his aberration.

He felt that everybody should know and appreciate him. Once, at Lord's, at the zenith of his career, he was bowling in an important match. Just to see what reaction and reprisal would result, a buddy of his wandered round to the score box, grabbed a little boy who was lurking there, gave him a sixpence and invited him to run almost on to the pitch and demand, in a loud voice, 'Bowler's name, please?'

The urchin concurred. Jackson was almost Jovian in his wrath. 'The impertinence! Fancy not knowing me at Lord's', he expostulated.

And he had as much confidence in other people as he had in himself. In 1897, when Yorkshire were playing against Somerset, the scoring of the few runs that Yorkshire required to win on the morning of the third day seemed a mere formality. So he and Frank Milligan, neither of whom had batted, decided to catch an early train and get a decent night's sleep before the next match.

From the window of the moving train they caught sight of the score-board on the county ground. Wickets had tumbled and Yorkshire were on the verge of defeat!

There were no pocket transistors in those days to give ball-by-ball commentaries. And what could have looked worse in the papers the next morning than that two officers and gentlemen had been absent without leave? The two truants endured an agonising journey to Leeds before they learnt that George Hirst and Schofie Haigh had dug their heels in and pulled the match out of the fire.

THE OFF-COMED CHUCKER

In Victorian times Lancashire was famous for its chuckers. In 1882, in his first season with Yorkshire, Lord Hawke complained that in the 'Roses' match he was twice bowled for a duck by Nash, whom he described as 'a real Lancashire chucker'. And, to rub salt into his wound, Alex Watson, another Lancastrian, remarked to Lord Hawke towards the end of his career, that he had chucked all his life and wasn't going to change at his age.

In 1885 Lord Harris, of Kent, decided to take a firm stand against illegal bowling and before Kent's game at Old Trafford he objected to both Nash and Crossland on the grounds that Crossland threw his fast ball and Nash every ball. When Lancashire declined to exclude them from their team for the return match, Lord Harris advised the Kent committee to decline to play and allow Lancashire to claim victory by default.

But Lord Harris did not always get his own way against Lancashire, who were eagerly awaiting a chance of revenge. Lord Harris had a keen eye for the proprieties of the game and, later, when S. S. Schultz was chosen to play for Lancashire against Kent, he objected, saying that Schultz had neither birth nor residential qualification for the county.

'But he has always played for Lancashire', 'Monkey' Hornby, the Lancashire captain, said.

Harris agreed but was adamant about his lack of qualification.

'His family home is in the county', insisted the Lancashire committee.

Lord Harris raised his eyebrows. 'Are you sure?' he inquired portentously, 'I understand that his mother lives in Birkenhead, and that is in Cheshire.'

'Ah, yes', agreed the Lancashire committee triumphantly. 'Cheshire it may be called in the South of England, but Birkenhead is part of the port of Liverpool.'

It was this preponderance of chuckers in Lancashire that ruined the hopes of H. J. Knutton of playing first-class cricket for Lancashire (for whom he had a residential qualification, having been professional for Little Lever, near Bolton) and perhaps of playing Test Match cricket for England. Lancashire refused to consider him, not because of his ability, but because 'they already had one chucker in their team', the reference no doubt, being to Mold who, at the turn of the century, was notorious for his bent arm delivery.

Knutton was captured from Little Lever by Abram Sowden, a staunch Yorkshireman, and brought to Bradford to be professional at Park Avenue. There he was outstanding, but, excepting for one game, was ostracised from first-class cricket. He played in one game only, but, in the only innings in which he bowled, he made a contribution which astonished the cricket world.

Australia had played Yorkshire at Bradford, and their itinerary included, next, a free date because of the Coronation of King Edward VII.

But the royal appendix caused the postponement of the crowning, the tourists were at a loose end, and a scratch team, styled 'North of England' was raised at short notice to play an extra three-day fixture at Bradford against the Australians. Although the tourists scored over 400 runs and won by an innings, Knutton

J. H. Knutton 'ostracised from first-class cricket'.
Inset *Knutton in action. W. G. complained that he was 'chucking'.*

performed the outstanding feat of taking nine wickets for a hundred runs.

Though admirers and contemporary club mates avowed there was 'nowt wrong with his bowling', Knutton was later to be penalised for his action, but it was a penalty of which he might well be proud, for it gave him the right to regard himself, if we exclude Ernie Jones, who bowled one through his beard, as the only man to intimidate W. G. Grace.

On a club tour of the South of England Bradford met London County at Crystal Palace and in Knutton's first over to the Doctor there was a snick, and Sandy Bairstow, Yorkshire's understudy to David Hunter, took the catch behind the wicket. That famous Yorkshire sportsman Ernest Holdsworth was fielding in the slips and was adamant that W. G. nearly knocked the cover off the ball.

But Dr. W G. Grace was not only the opening batsman for London County. He was originator, instigator, organiser, president, chairman, committee, manager, advertising agent and captain of the club. No umpire gave W. G. out at Crystal Palace with impunity. A deaf ear was turned to the exultant appeal.

At the end of the over the Doctor approached the umpire to advise him that Knutton was throwing and should be taken off. The umpire acquiesced. Knutton bowled no more in the match, and no more in first-class cricket . . . and W. G. went on to score an immaculate century.

When his playing days were over, H. J. Knutton opened a sports outfitter's shop. Breaker of the rules of cricket he may have been, but in his business dealings the odour of Victorian sanctity and a reluctance to mention parts of the human form remained.

Once, during the cricket season, when he was old but still active, I went into his shop and asked for a bodyguard.

A mother and her small son were at the counter buying a ludo set or a bagatelle board. Quickly H. J. nipped round the counter, took my arm and led me away to a storeroom. Carefully he closed the door, looked at me quizzically, put both his hands over the part of the anatomy I intended to protect, and looked at me questioningly. I nodded in agreement.

He took one out of a cupboard, wrapped it up and gave it to me. 'Young man', he said, when we had completed the transaction, 'you must not ask for things like that in my shop when there are ladies present.'

Today his is just a name over a Bradford shop. With better luck it might have been a name written large in *Wisden*.

O my Emmett and my Wainwright long ago

Right *Dr. W. G. Grace on his 65th birthday in 1913.*

Below *From the left: A. Sellers, E. Smith, Lord Hawke and the Hon. F. S. Jackson.*

Above Tom Emmett, cricket's clown prince.

Above left G. H. Hirst, as drawn by 'Spy' in 1903.

Left Yorkshire team of 1901. Behind: E. Wainwright, L. Whitehead, W. Rhodes, D. Hunter; middle row: G. H. Hirst, 'Mr.' E. Smith, Lord Hawke, 'Mr.' F. Mitchell, J. Tunnicliffe; front row: D. Denton, 'Mr.' T. L. Taylor and J. T. Brown.

Schofield Haigh, equal as a bowler with Hirst and Rhodes.

NEGLECTED HERO

Biographers have dealt kindly, sometimes even obsequiously, with Hirst and Rhodes. Their niche in cricket mythology is secure. Nevertheless, the effusions of these historians and the passage of time have linked them too closely. Granted that they were the two greatest all-round cricketers of all time; that both came from the same Yorkshire village of Kirkheaton, near Huddersfield; that both bowled left arm and batted right; that for 20 years they were contemporaries in the county team. Yet they were not David and Jonathan, Darby and Joan, Dick and Liddy or whatever other pair of inseparables wishful thinking has compared them with. When a celebration match was arranged to honour Rhodes's seventieth birthday and Wilfred was going to bowl the first over of the game, George was asked if he was going to watch. 'No', he said. A pause, then, drily, he added, 'Ah've seen him bowl afore, tha knaws.'

Whether the praise of Hirst and Rhodes has been over-fulsome or not, it has certainly detracted from the memory of one, who, for 15 years, was their contemporary in the Yorkshire team; one who was also a Huddersfield lad, who was their equal as a bowler, and, who, if his batting was not quite on a par with theirs, was nevertheless good enough to score centuries and to achieve the 'double'.

Hirst and Rhodes, for all their greatness, were merely two legs of the tripod. The third member was Schofield Haigh, one of the greatest off-spin bowlers who has ever lived. Although his last season was 1913, he still holds the record of having obtained more of his wickets clean-bowled than any other first-class cricketer. But, alas, Schofie died at 49. Ripe old age did not for him confer the aura of mystery and perfection that hallowed George and Wilfred.

After a rainy night he would saunter out to the middle, thumb the pitch, return to the pavilion and, with a wicked grin, announce to his captain, 'They'll deviate this morning, mi lord', though where a Huddersfield had learnt the word *deviate* is almost as big a mystery as where Schofie acquired his prodigious off-break.

His Test career was spread over a period of 13 years, although he was never the automatic choice that Wilfred was for so long, and George for a shorter period. Even more than Hirst he rejoiced in playing for Yorkshire but could raise less enthusiasm for Test cricket, and he suffered from the failure of Test captains to appreciate his foible of detesting a new ball. Yet although he took only 24 Test wickets they were cheaper than either George's and Wilfred's.

He was a great lover of cricket and did all he could for the good of the game, sometimes attempting tasks beyond his capacity. Once, as a young Yorkshire player, he felt greatly honoured when he was asked to present the prizes to a local team at an annual dinner. Determined to do well, he went into solemn conclave with his father and, with much heart-searching, hammered out a suitable speech.

On the evening of the gathering, Schofie ascended the platform and was introduced to the chairman. In dismay he looked at the sea of faces before him. Then he addressed them. 'When Ah came on to this platform', he said, 'nobbut me and mi fayther knew what Ah were bahn to say. And nah nobbut mi fayther knaws.'

In a rich, Yorkshire dialect he would tell his favourite cricket stories, recalling, for instance, a village match in the days of his youth, when equipment was scarce. The opposing team had only pads enough for the batsmen to wear one each, and, in such unfortunate cases, it is worn on the front batting leg. When a batsman came in with the single pad on his right leg, the fielding side naturally assumed he was a left hander and took up their positions accordingly. But when he got to the wicket and took up his stance he was a right-hander. 'Tha's getten thi pad on t'wreng leg', a fieldsman pointed out. Surprised, the batsman glanced down. 'Oh, aye, so Ah hev', he exclaimed. 'Ah thought Ah were battin' at t' other end.'

Some remarkable performances stand to Schofield's credit. On five occasions, in 1902, 1905, 1906, 1908 and 1909, he was top of the All England bowling averages. In 1901 he and Wilfred bowled Nottinghamshire out for 13. In 1908 Northamptonshire were admitted to the County Championship for the first time. Their first match was against Yorkshire. Schofie and George bowled them out for 27 in the first innings and 15 in the second.

His first great bowling performance was 8 for 33 against Warwickshire in 1898; his last, 6 for 14 against the Australians in 1912.

When he was not chosen for the 1902 Test Match against the Australians his non-inclusion was described as an irreparable mistake on the part of the Selection Committee. Someone had surely blundered, it was declared, leaving out a man whose bowling many first-class batsmen had in several matches pronounced as unplayable.

He took 1,916 wickets for Yorkshire, and only Hirst and Rhodes have exceeded that number. He performed the hat-trick three times. In 1898 at Bradford he and George had a record ninth wicket partnership of 192.

Whether the praise given to George and Wilfred has been too effusive is arguable, but certainly the ignoring of Schofield Haigh has been unwarrantable.

MASTERMIND

Lord Hawke was a blue-blooded aristocrat. He held, in 1897, the position in the British Empire that was regarded as second only to monarchy. He was captain of Yorkshire cricket.

Bobby Peel was a great Test Match cricketer, the star of the North. Loaded with years and honours, he was a Yorkshire folk hero. But on one occasion Bobby strayed from the strict path of rectitude that his lordship laid down for his players. With no more conpunction than he would have felt in dealing with an under-housemaid at his stately home, Lord Hawke dismissed him.

The loss of their star in no way worried Yorkshire. At the start of the 1898 season, on the morning of the first match against the MCC at Lord's, Lord Hawke turned to one of his minions and said, 'Jacker' (and this, mark you, not to a ground boy, but to the Honourable Francis Stanley Jackson, later Sir Stanley Jackson, BA, Cant., Hon. D. Litt., Knight of Grace of St. John of Jerusalem, M.P., Financial Secretary to the War Office, Governor of Bengal), 'Jacker', he said, almost casually, 'I have two colts here, Rhodes and Cordingley. Let them bowl at you in the nets'.

So they bowled, and after his practical observation of their respective abilities, the Hon. Stanley chose Rhodes to fill the one vacancy in the Yorkshire team.

The MCC had a powerful team, including W. G. Grace, captain of England and W. L. Murdoch, captain of Australia, but Wilfred Rhodes took four wickets for 24 runs, and in his first county match took 13 wickets. 'He tortured the batsmen with scorpions', said one report, commenting on his 154 wickets in his first season.

This was not the Rhodes we came to know after the First World War, the bowler of the slow, flighted, cunning delivery. 'He bowls left-hand medium', said W. G. Grace, 'with a good break and an action that is both easy and graceful. On slow wickets he is deadly, and on fast, hard wickets batsmen have difficulty in getting him away.'

Some denigrated his ability, saying that it had been a season of bowlers' wickets and that he would be tamed when hard wickets arrived. But next season 'critics and prophets were put to silence when, in a batsman's year, he took 150 wickets for 16 runs apiece, or as many wickets as any two bowlers on his side'.

So the acclamation of the country for his wonderful bowling rang in his ears, while he went to bed and dreamed of the day he would be a great batsman.

At the turn of the century it was felt that a ball should respond to a bowler's hand like a violin in Yehudi Menuhin's fingers. If the bowler scored runs he would lose his bowling touch and the ball would be no more alive in his palm than a lump of dough. So Lord Hawke worried and sent Wilfred in at number 11 with the exhortation, that he should score no more than 20, to which, at Leyton, Wilfred once wistfully replied that he hoped some day to play for England for his batting. He then proceeded, with the straightest of straight bats and the skill of an opening batsman, to reach his alloted span.

In three seasons he took 725 wickets. In 1902, in the Test Match at Birmingham, he took seven wickets for 17 runs when the Australians were bowled out for 36. In

Top *Lord Hawke (left) and Wilfred Rhodes in 1908.*
Below *Rhodes in old age with friends Herbert Sutcliffe and Norman Hazell.*

the winter of 1903-1904, at Melbourne, he took 15 wickets against Australia, but more to his liking was the 40 runs not out he made going in last and helping R. E. Foster in a record last wicket stand of 130.

But, just as Lord Hawke had feared, as his batting improved, his bowling deteriorated. He could still get his 100 wickets a season to add to the 1,500 runs he was scoring, but, gradually, batting superseded bowling. In 1911-1912 again he was in Australia. His bowling was regarded as of little consequence, for by then he was England's opening batsman, sharing with Jack Hobbs in a record opening stand of 323 at Melbourne.

He was in the middle thirties. He had reached his goal, the zenith of his ambition. No more conquests seemed possible.

Then came the First World War. Major Booth and Alonzo Drake, two of Yorkshire's great young bowlers, were lost to cricket; other players had withered with the passage of time. Although he was nearly forty-three years old, like a fond grandfather with a brood of orphans, Wilfred gathered the inexperienced Yorkshire players around him. He picked up again the art of slow bowling that he had so disdainfully abandoned. He batted with a correctness and exactitude that were an example to the young men who were privileged to dress in the same pavilion. In seven more seasons he achieved the cricketer's double of 1,000 runs and 100 wickets in a season.

In 1926 he became a Test Match selector. At international level English cricket was in a sorry state. As the last game of the season approached, only one out of the last nineteen Test Matches against Australia had been won, and a formidable eleven, which included Woodfull, Bardsley, Macartney, Ponsford, Gregory, Grimmett and Mailey, was poised to take the Ashes back to Australia.

So, on a Sunday morning in London, when the Test Selection Committee met to discuss this dire emergency, Wilfred was resurrected. He had first played for England before three of the team were born. In the first innings he bowled 25 overs for 35 runs (and two wickets). In the second, on a rain-affected wicket, they were at his mercy. He took four wickets for 44 runs, and England won by 289 runs.

In the Yorkshire team, his mantle had passed to Roy Kilner, accurate as a bowler, punishing as a batsman, in the prime of his career.

Now, it must have seemed, Wilfred could sing his Nunc Dimittis; but before the start of the 1928 season Roy Kilner had died in Barnsley Fever Hospital.

Again Wilfred took up the reins. Hedley Verity was discovered. Painstakingly Wilfred nurtured him till another Yorkshire left-arm bowler was ready for England.

Although Wilfred was proud of his success, his praise, in Verity's presence, was grudging. Once, in Verity's formative years, he bowled well to take seven wickets for 28 runs. After the match Rhodes approached Verity, who waited eagerly for the shower of congratulation. 'You bowled very well today, Hedley', Wilfred condescended, 'and you bowled one ball that I could never manage to bowl all my life.' 'Which was that?' asked the entranced Verity. 'That short one they hit past square leg for four', said Wilfred. For Wilfred Rhodes averred that, throughout his career, he was never hooked and never cut.

In old age fate dealt scurvily with him. For many years he was blind, but his enthusiasm for all the skills and intricacies of the game never wavered.

As he sat in the pavilion one day at a county match with a Huddersfield administrator, a wicket fell to the last ball of an over and Ted Lester came in to bat.

After a few minutes Wilfred turned to his friend and said, 'What is Lester doing now?' 'He's at the non-striker's end', came the explanation. 'I know that', said Wilfred, 'but what is he doing?' 'He isn't doing anything', was the nonplussed answer. Wilfred was astonished, 'Isn't he watching the bowler's run-up, noticing his action, finger spin, speed and length?'

On July 9 1973, at the age of ninety-five, Wilfred died. Today first-class cricket has emasculated itself to suit the speed and love of gold of the modern world. It may, in the future, thrown up fleeting heroes, but the last of Yorkshire's gods has gone to his cricketing Valhalla.

THE LIKELY LAD FROM LAWKHOLME

A cult fostered and fomented by Neville Cardus was instigated 40 or 50 years ago to raise or demean Emmott Robinson to the status of a wag, a clown, a Yorkshire comedian. No more humourless cricketer ever walked the face of the earth.

Henley may have regarded himself as master of his fate and captain of his soul, but not so Emmott. He felt himself pursued by a malevolent destiny, a treacherous demon whose pleasures were annoyance, antagonism and, ultimately, destruction.

In the later years of his life Emmott lived in a small terrace house near to Bradford's city centre and spent much of his lonely time in the reading room of the Mechanics Institute.

Sitting talking to me there one evening he pulled a medicine bottle from his waistcoat pocket, carefully took off the screw top and put a small white pill into his mouth.

Anxiously I asked him, 'Aren't you so well, Emmott?' He nodded thoughtfully. 'It's my stomach', he said, and then, after a pause, be added, 'It's Wilfred's fault.'

Now we have it on the word of George Hirst himself that Wilfred Rhodes had mighty digestive organs. In the Golden Age of Cricket there reigned at Lord's P. F. Warner, a great batsman, a Test Match captain, the first man to score a century in the West Indies, and, later in life, when bald as a King of Siam, incomparable administrator, chairman of Test selectors, *eminence grise* of the Marylebone Cricket Club.

But Pelham, 'Plum' to his intimates, suffered from gastric trouble and often, on important occasions, this incapacitated him severely.

Once, when Middlesex were playing Yorkshire, instead of coming in at number four as was his wont, Plum had lain prostrate throughout the sunny afternoon on the pavilion table. But, bravely, as the ninth wicket fell, he climbed to his feet, buckled on his pads and, his face wan with pain, struggled unsteadily to the middle. Kindly George Hirst, for in all things George was a kindly man, went up to him and commiserated on his illness. 'Ee, Mr. Warner', he concluded, 'if thou'd nobbut had a stomach like me and Wilfred thou'd have broken t'hearts of every bowler in t'world.'

Yes, Wilfred had a mighty stomach and often, in winter, between the Wars when he was not touring with an MCC side, he went to India as a kind of paid guest to the estate of some nawab, maharajah or nizam, acting as professional coach to the prince's cricket team, and also, no doubt, as autocratic captain while His Highness officially held the title.

Along with him, for company no doubt, as obviously he would require no help in bowling out the prince's enemies, Wilfred took another Yorkshire cricketer and one year invited Emmott to accompany him. Now Wilfred, besides having a mighty stomach, had a strong distaste for wasting money . . .

Slowly Emmott slipped the medicine bottle back into his pocket. 'We used to live in a corner of t'pavilion', he said, 'and looked after ussen. We'd been warned not to buy owt to eat in t'Indian market but t'village wasn't far away and chickens were cheap there so Wilfred used to slip out and buy one. It were one o'them that upset my stomach and it's never been reyt since. When I got back home I said I hoped I'd never see another Indian as long as I lived.'

But since that day a migratory revolution has taken place in the sub-continent. Indians and Pakistanis have swarmed into the Yorkshire textile mills, the Leicester hosiery factories, the Black Country and the London boroughs, occupying the town centres. Emmott, looking out of the window into Town Hall Square, waved his arm forlornly as if to embrace the whole of the inner ring of Bradford. 'And now look what's happened', he complained, 'they've come to live all round me.'

His cricket life throughout had been a struggle. He was in his mid-thirties before joining the County team, a dilatoriness he blamed on the selection committee who, he felt, frowned on the fact that a Yorkshireman was playing as a league professional with a Lancashire club.

But he did valiant service in Lancashire, overcoming by ability the natural

Emmott Robinson, 'pursued by a malevolent destiny'.

hostility to Yorkshiremen in the county and particularly the odium a former Yorkshire professional had engendered that led almost to ostracism.

For a predecessor of Emmott's, having, one Saturday afternoon, performed his duties to the best of his considerable ability, was met as he walked off the field by the club treasurer who remarked, as if it were of no consequence, 'I'm sorry. We haven't enough brass to pay thee with today, lad. I'll see tha gets it next Saturday.'

Now, while this derisory, inconsequential attitude to a man's contracted emolument may pass muster in Lancashire, Yorkshiremen simply cannot countenance such casual behaviour. And thereafter, every Saturday, the aggrieved Yorkshire professional changed into his flannels and before he took the field sought out the club treasurer, demanded and received his fee.

But what, now, to do with the money? If he left it in the pavilion, like a good Tyke not trusting Lancastrians, he suspected, light-fingered gentlemen might enter the changing room while he was batting or bowling and remove his hard-earned wages.

He had come prepared for this. He folded the pound notes and slipped them down the inside of his sock, produced from his pocket a black elastic garter and twisting this round his calf safely imprisoned the money. And there it stayed until evening when he was safely back in his native West Riding and could remove it in the seclusion of his bedroom.

But back to Emmott, now in his mid-thirties, prematurely grey, seamed and wizened of countenance, timber-toed and wearing flannels that, if they were not hitched up persistently, wrinkled in concertinas round his boots. Looking like a prospect for a geriatric ward, he entered the Yorkshire team to give over a decade of yeoman service. He opened the bowling with his medium fast outswingers, batted boldly in the middle of the order, fielded suicidally at forward short leg.

He was standing there once when a young amateur playing for a Southern county came in to bat. The youth surveyed the field, espied this grandfatherly figure within touching distance of the bat and invited him, in the interests of his personal safety, to withdraw from the firing line. Emmott stood his ground. 'Thee get on wi' thi batting, lad', he advised, 'an' Ah'll mind missen and mi fielding.'

His buddy in the Yorkshire team was Wilfred Rhodes. Between them existed a sort of love-hate relationship. Both were great students of the game and gave much time to silent thought and quiet discussion. Envious colleagues, aware that both were loth to spend their money, suggested that they spent more time contemplating their stocks and shares than Philip Mead's leg glance or Frank Woolley's cover drive.

But whether they agreed on financial matters or not, they were often at variance in their estimation of cricket ability.

Once, when Wilfred was a member of the Test Selection Committee and England were not doing too well against Australia, Emmott gave vent to his thoughts. 'What yo' want', he explained to Wilfred, 'is a slow spin bowler. Somebody like Dick Tyldesley. You'll hev to pick a spin bowler for t'next Test.'

'Aye,' agreed Wilfred, 'we s'all pick a spin bowler for t'next Test. But it'll nooan be Dick Tyldesley. Ah'm bahn to pick missen.'

On another occasion, at Leyton, it had rained heavily during the night. Wilfred went out to inspect the wicket and, coming back, announced, 'If we win t'toss we mun put 'em in to bat. We shall bowl Essex aht for 90.'

This expert opinion was not good enough for Emmott. He also proceeded to the middle, prodded the pitch, spoke to the groundsman, thumbed the run-ups, and strolled back. 'Nay, Wilfred', he opined, 'thou'rt wrong. Ah reckon they'll get 93.'

It lies in the power of every cricketer to bowl the unplayable ball. We met it often when we were little boys playing in the setted streets. It hit the corner of a sett, then, in the words of Schofield Haigh, 'deviated' and down went your middle wicket. Imitating the words of the likely lads in the Sunday school cricket team second eleven when they failed to orientate their bats in the same vertical plane as the dipping ball, we retired disconsolately, murmuring, 'It'd hev bowled Jack Hobbs'.

But a first-class wicket at Lord's or Old Trafford is not a setted street, and except for Sydney Barnes, who, on average, bowled it three times an over, few bowlers produced that ball more than once a season, and, when it happened, hoped that facing them was at least Syd Gregory, Ranjitsinghi or Victor Trumper.

At Fenners, playing against the University, with the last two men at the wicket, Emmott produced this special. It pitched on the leg stump, whipped across and took the off bail. The undergraduate contemplated his wicket, walked out, and, as all polite youths should, said to Emmott as he passed, 'Oh, what a good ball'. Emmott surveyed the scene. In the words of our youth, 'It would have bowled Jack Hobbs', and the victim had been a University rabbit! 'Aye', replied Emmott to the youth in disgust, 'it were. But it were wasted on thee.'

Even when success smiled on him he was rarely given his full due. In 1920, at Bradford's Park Avenue, Yorkshire were in imminent danger of defeat against Lancashire, but in the second innings, while Waddington was getting 0 for 54, Rhodes 0 for 27 and Macaulay 0 for 18, Emmott took the first nine wickets for 36 runs and enabled Yorkshire to win by 22 runs. The margin was too narrow to allow sentiment to creep in and Roy Kilner took the last wicket, robbing Emmott of the cherished 'All Ten'.

Later, talking to Roy Kilner, a supporter who had not been at the match, said, 'You did well to beat 'em. Who bowled 'em out?'

'Oh', answered Roy airily, 'me and Emmott.'

We sat again in the Mechanics Institute. It was the last time I saw Emmott. We had been discussing the few years he spent in the North Eastern Leagues after his county career had ended.

'They tell me', I said, 'that you bowled off-spinners.'

He nodded in agreement.

'But when you played for Yorkshire you always bowled out-swingers.' Again he nodded.

'Tell me', I persisted, 'didn't you ever bowl an off-spinner when you played with Yorkshire?'

'No', he said, 'never one.' He paused for a minute lost in thought as if there were passing in front of him a whole life of forbidden opportunities. 'Tha sees', he explained, 'if ivver I'd made one spin for Yorkshire they'd hev taken me off straight away and put Wilfred on.'

IMMACULATE BULWARK

Herbert Sutcliffe, who died on January 22 1978 at the age of eighty-three, was a member of that merciless and militant band who, high-handed and immutably determined, ruled English cricket between the two World Wars. Yet with his debonair appearance, film star good looks and diplomatic demeanour, he hardly resembled his fellows.

Drawn from the mills and the pits, tousled in appearance, piratical in execution, broad in the beam and in dialect, insular in outlook, they were a close-knit band of warriors that one attribute alone could have compelled to accept into their brotherhood so obvious a misfit. But this the misfit had in abundance: ability, coupled with such doggedness and determination that when the enemy loomed large and defeat threatened to overwhelm the brotherhood, he was not only a sturdy colleague but their Horatius who held, defiantly, the centre of the bridge. Perhaps his whole philosophy of life was summed up in the short statement he made when Pelham Warner congratulated him on rescuing England from ignoble defeat. 'Mr. Warner', he smiled in satisfaction, 'I love a dog fight.'

He came into the Yorkshire team at the end of the First War, batting in the middle of the order: but Wilfred Rhodes, who was opening the innings, was, as a great batsman, past his prime if not approaching senility, and the gaps left by the tragic deaths of Major Booth and Alonzo Drake meant that Wilfred was required as a master bowler. Rhodes was not sorry to change places with Sutcliffe, whose philosophy was always to regard himself as *nullus secundus*.

Thus he began with Percy Holmes a batting partnership that became the most celebrated in county cricket. Lantern-jawed, his cap rakishly set, Percy Holmes brought an impish devilry to his batting. Improvising with an armoury full of self-taught tactics, he devastated his opponents.

In immaculate composure, Sutcliffe watched from the other end. Percy was his senior but not his mentor. Nobody was Sutcliffe's mentor. He batted with classic regality, imperious perfection. There was no gap between bat and pad for the off-break to sneak through; there was no stretched out, lunging bat that allowed the away swinger to nibble at the edge. There was the certitude of correct batsmanship, untempted into error by guile, and here, when the struggle became tense, when the ball reared intimidatingly, was the bastion which humbled England's and Yorkshire's jealous foes. When the sun shone he was a great batsman but when the tempest roared he was greater still.

Never flamboyant, never mercurial, only when the bowlers tried to unnerve him did he show the terrible truculence that lurked below the surface of his calm. Once, at Scarborough, Kenneth Farnes of Essex, at that time possibly the fastest bowler in England, decided in boyish impetuosity that it might be stimulating to attempt to knock Herbert's block off. Sutcliffe and Maurice Leyland chastised the youth by taking over one hundred runs off him in seven overs.

'Nobody likes it, but some show it more than others', had been Leyland's laconic comment when asked about fast and dangerous bowling. He had forgotten Herbert. Sutcliffe revelled in it.

Sutcliffe hits a boundary in a Test match at the Oval in 1934.

'The perfect second string', an obituarist called him. Nothing could be further from the truth. Just because it was Holmes and Sutcliffe for Yorkshire and Hobbs and Sutcliffe for England, Herbert in no way regarded himself as the lesser light. Second he might be, but only in seniority, and once, against South Africa, when Hobbs was absent and Holmes was promoted to the England team, Sutcliffe, having spoken long and earnestly to his captain, saw with satisfaction that the English batting order read, 'Sutcliffe and Holmes'.

Do we need figures? Statistics may not lie but rarely, unfortunately, do they more than touch on the truth. They do not show the effort, the heartache, the joy, the dismay, the glory, the misery of human toil. Nevertheless . . . Sutcliffe made more runs in first-class cricket than any other Yorkshireman. He played in fifty-four Test Matches. He is reputed to have made every score between 0 and 126. If this is true (and I have no intention of wading through twenty *Wisdens* to check it) he is more deserving than many to enter Guinness's magic book.

He shared with Percy Holmes in the record first wicket stand of 555 against Essex in 1932. Now, about this, and perhaps telling tales out of school, the previous record was 554 by two other Yorkshiremen, Brown and Tunnicliffe, in the dim and distant past. As Yorkshire passed this mighty total, in the easing of the tension, a wicket fell. Then, staggeringly, incredibly, the score board was changed back to 554. Uproar, excursion and alarm followed. Mentally jogged by every man in Leyton, where the match was played, the scorers searched through the figures.

Cynics doubtless wondered whether they were truthful or merely wise. But a no-ball was found, the record was restored and joy reigned unalloyed.

Nobody seems to have asked Sutcliffe's opinion. Nowadays a dozen microphones would be thrust under his nose. Perhaps they were wise in their generation. Perhaps they remembered a former occasion when George Hirst had completed some mighty feat requiring much sweat and toil. 'How do you feel about it, Mr. Hirst?' he had been asked ingenuously. Sardonically George looked at his questioner. 'Varry tired', he had replied.

As time marches on many find their way into records, more into ghosted autobiography, but few are honoured by contemporary literature. There was written, when I was a lad, *Test Match Surprise* (out of print, publishers Woolworths, now priceless, original price 6d.).

It was an epic of glorious cricketing endeavour. When I was 'at home' I treasured it behind the glass window of the bookcase in my tiny bedroom, but, alas, there came to me, as to all red-blooded youths in those days, that sorry moment when, quite erroneously, I felt that marriage was more important than cricket, I took to myself a wife. In the flitting, my lovely book disappeared.

Vaguely I remember the book. The hero was Geoffrey Riversdale, son of Lord Riversdale. He did, if I remember rightly, bowl out the Australians, save the family fortunes and win a beautiful bride. But that was of little importance. Who were these who were opening England's innings? Who were those who were taking the spite and edge off the Australian speed merchants? Why, Ratcliffe and Sherlock. Ratcliffe and Sherlock? Rubbish. It was Herbert and Percy.

And so I remember them. Sutcliffe and Holmes. Ratcliffe and Sherlock. Neither in life nor in literature did they fail when the chips were down.

Maurice Leyland – 'delightful humour'.

THE 'CROSS BAT VILLAGE GREENER'

By the waters of Jordan the mantle of Elijah fell and was taken up by Elisha. There was no such visual manifestation in the 1920s, but just as surely the spirit of George Hirst descended on Maurice Leyland; not in his physical ability to discountenance batsmen with his violent swerve or venomously to thump the ball to square leg, but in his kindness, thoughtfulness, courtesy and his love of Yorkshire cricket and its way of life.

Maurice first entered the compact, inviolate circle of the Yorkshire team in 1920. After he had played a few games for the county a committee man asked a senior player how he was getting on. 'Oh, all reyt', was the non-committal answer. 'Aye, well', said the committee man, incensed at this lack of enthusiasm, 'you'd better get used to him, because he's bahn to be with you for a long time.' As he was, till 1946.

At the end of the 1928 season an England team was to be chosen to tour Australia. One of the difficulties facing the Selection Committee was which two left-hand batsmen to take.

In the last season peerless Frank Woolley, the Pride of Kent, had scored 3,352 runs with an average of 61; Philip Mead of Hampshire, immovable as a barnacle, 3,027 with an average of 75, and Leyland 1,783 runs, average 54.

In spite of the figures, Woolley was left out and, it was said, 'a wail went up from Gravesend to Dover'. Woolley was said to be a 'god', while Mead was a 'leaden-footed cart-horse', and Leyland 'a cross bat village greener'.

It was strange that after all this disagreement and dissatisfaction Mead played only in the first Test and Leyland in the final one. But when, at last, Leyland was given his chance in Australia he scored 137 in the first innings and 53 not out in the second.

Until the Second World War he was an automatic choice for England, and we are apt to forget that when England made their record score of 903 for seven wickets, declared, at the Oval against Australia in 1938, a score dominated by Hutton's record 364, Leyland scored 187 before being run out, he and Hutton having taken the score from 29 to 411.

But more than his 26,000 runs and 400 wickets, his 1,000 runs a season for 17 consecutive years from 1923 to 1939, his 62 centuries for Yorkshire and his 41 Test Matches, it is his humanity, spice, generosity and goodwill that shine through his career.

At the outbreak of the Second World War he was 39, but immediately joined the Army. In the summer of 1942, as a sergeant instructor, he was stationed at Bradford. Benefit matches for the Forces were being played at Leeds, but Maurice refused to take part because he suspected that professional cricketers playing in these matches were being paid for their services and this was repugnant to him.

For a prestigious Bank Holiday match the organiser wrote to Maurice's commanding officer asking for Maurice's release to play in the match.

The C.O. sent for Maurice. 'Sergeant Leyland', he said, passing the letter across his table, 'I have had this request and given permission for you to play.'

'Aye, well', said Maurice, returning the letter. 'I shan't play in that match. But I've a letter here from Kent asking if I can play there in a benefit match on the same day. It says no fees and no expenses of any kind will be paid. I'll go there if you'll give me the day off.'

He had a delightful, pawky sense of humour and loved telling his Yorkshire tales, probably apocryphal and invariably poking fun at himself. One he enjoyed repeating was that one winter's evening when he was a senior member of both Yorkshire and England and was at the height of his fame, sitting in the front room with his wife, he took out a bat, oiled it and then, standing on the rug, played one or two practice shots. His wife looked up at him from her sewing. 'Ee, Maurice', she said in surprise, 'do you bat left-handed?'

Once he was asked by an important cricket reporter what it felt like to go out to bat in a Test Match. 'Well', said Maurice contemplatively, 'it isn't very pleasant. You walk down the pavilion steps; you're going in to bat against the best bowler in the world: there's 30,000 people watching you, and they all know better than you how to play him.'

Inevitably, at the end of his playing days, he became coach to the county. It is a post as important to Yorkshire cricket as that of Cantuar to the Church of England. For, besides searching out and developing dormant talent, he must, by sagacity, humour, wisdom, kindness and heroic tales of derring-do, implant the glory, not of individual performance, but of a century of endeavour, success and pride.

If spirits are allowed to haunt their earthly paradises, then the happy ghosts of George Hirst and Maurice Leyland, with twinkling smiles and stocky figures, will wander proudly on the pitch at Headingley when, in the Whitsuntide Roses match, the Lancashire wickets are falling to their White Rose successors.

'We shall not see their like again . . . ' Lord Hawke's 'great Champion County team'. Back row: E. Smith, Rhodes, Whitehead, Hunter; middle row: Wainwright, T. L. Taylor, Lord Hawke, Tunnicliffe, Hirst; front row: Denton, Brown, Haigh.

EPILOGUE

We shall not see their like again. Cricket has been immolated to the God of Gold and the titillation of spectators; to popularising the game for every yobbo who can wave a flag, blow a trumpet or rattle an empty beer can.

We limit the overs, cover the wicket and change the ball every hour or so rather than, as William Gunn so succinctly put it, 'play with one till t'bloddy cover drops off'.

For the true joy now we must retreat to the village cricket fields, where mothers and sweethearts sweat away their Saturday afternoons over bubbling, antiquated tea urns, buttering potted meat sandwiches, slicing sponge cakes surmounted by lions couchant, selling Shrewsbury biscuits decorated with cochineal; where fathers reverently watch their offspring, quick to jump to their support at the slightest hint of outside criticism; vociferously pointing out to them, from the boundary edge, every flaw in length, every deviation from the straight bat; where little boys, still learning to count on their fingers, rush for the honour of putting up the score tins, so that sometimes we are regaled with the improbability of seven runs for 15 wickets, last man 794.

And I, hidden in a faraway corner, gently suck my pipe and watch and watch, hoping against hope to see a reincarnation of Wilfred, a swerve as vehement as George's, an off-break as prodigious as Schofie's, or the hook of a short ball as regal as Herbert's.

Sadly I shake my head. There is no resurrection of my old heroes. The Yorkshire giants are forgotten by all but me, and yet . . .

Surprisingly, astonishingly, in 1979, to popularise its phone-in service for Test Match scores, the Post Office began a Press advertising campaign using cartoons of cricketers of the Golden Age.

First came Dr. Grace and who could argue with that? Soon we should see Stanley Jackson, Martin Hawke, Wilfred Rhodes, Georgie Hirst gracing, once more, the newspaper columns.

But the next two . . . Who were they? I peered in disbelief. Lord Dalmeny and Captain Edward Wynyard. Who, in Yorkshire, or for that matter, anywhere else, except perhaps at Lord's, had ever heard of them?

There was no doubt where my duty lay: to write immediately to the Prime Minister, demanding the resignation or dismissal, with ignominy, of the Post Master General, and, at once, to launch a Yorkshire Separatist campaign, so that once more, as in the halcyon days of Edwin, Oswald, Ossy and St. Paulinus, we should be the master of our own fate.

My letter was drafted and ready for posting when the fourth cartoon appeared . . . and there he was with his cheerful smile and rubicund complexion, our own George Hirst.

Slowly I tore up my letter and dropped it into the fire, my despondency gone. For I was dreaming hopefully of the next season, when England would be represented by Yorkshire, when the Post Office would feature our long-gone giants, Stanley, Schofie, Martin, Wilfred, Ted Peate, Bobby Peel, George Ulyett, John Tunnicliffe . . . that glorious band that, as surely as the Royal Navy, once made Britain Great.

Also from The Whitethorn Press . . .

Queer Folk
by Maurice Colbeck.
A comicality of Yorkshire characters.
£1.85. By post £2.10.

Yorkshire Laughter
by Maurice Colbeck.
A further comicality from the Broad Acres.
£1.85. By post £2.10.

Queer Goings On
by Maurice Colbeck.
Yet another Yorkshire comicality.
£1.85. By post £2.05.

Steam-up in Lancashire
Railwayana from *Lancashire Life*.
£1.00. By post £1.25.

Just Sithabod
Dialect verse from *Lancashire Life*.
£1.50. By post £1.65.

Cheyp at t'Price
More dialect verse from *Lancashire Life*.
£1.50. By post £1.65.

Flower Arrangement - Free Style
by Edith Brack.
£2.20. By post £2.45.

And, every month, the magazines:
Yorkshire Life
Cheshire Life
Lancashire Life
Gloucestershire & Avon Life
Warwickshire & Worcestershire Life

The Whitethorn Press Ltd., P.O. Box 237, Thomson House,
Withy Grove, Manchester M60 4BL.
And 33-35, Cross Green, Otley LS21 1HD.